100 POSTWAR POEMS

1OO POSTWAR POEMS

British and American

Edited by

M. L. ROSENTHAL

The Macmillan Company, New York

First Printing

Library of Congress catalog card number: 68–12074

Printed in the United States of America

Acknowledgments

A. Alvarez, "Operation," by permission of the author.

Astor-Honor, Inc. "Icos," from *Seeing Is Believing*, by Charles Tomlinson. © copyright 1958 by Charles Tomlinson. Reprinted by permission of Astor-Honor, Inc., New York, New York, 10017.

Atheneum House, Inc. Randall Jarrell, "Windows," from *The Woman at the Washington Zoo* by Randall Jarrell. Copyright © 1960 by Randall Jarrell. Michael Hamburger, "Security," and "Homage to the Weather." From *Weather and Season* by Michael Hamburger. Copyright © 1963 by Michael Hamburger. Reprinted by permission of Atheneum Publishers.

Paul Blackburn, "Málaga: port," by permission of the author.

Chatto & Windus Ltd. Norman MacCaig, "Innocence" from *The Sinai Sort* (1957), and "Near Midnight" from *Surroundings* (1966). Jon Silkin, "Someone I Lost" from *The Two Freedoms* (1958). Reprinted by permission of Chatto & Windus Ltd.

Chilmark Press Inc. Richard Murphy, "Girl at the Seaside," from *Sailing to an Island*, © Richard Murphy, 1963—Chilmark Press.

Christy & Moore, Ltd. Dannie Abse, "After the Release of Ezra Pound," from *Poems Golders Green* (1962). Reprinted by permission of Christy & Moore, Ltd.

City Lights Books. Allen Ginsberg, "Proem: I" from *Kaddish*. Copyright © 1961 by Allen Ginsberg. Reprinted by permission of City Lights Books.

iv

Corinth Books, Inc. Charles Olson, "Maximus, to Himself." From *The Maximus Poems* © 1960 Charles Olson. Published by Jargon Books in association with Corinth Books, Inc. Gary Snyder, "Logging." From *Myths and Texts* © 1960 Gary Snyder. Published by Token Press in association with Corinth Books, Inc.

Curtis Brown, Ltd. Donald Hall, "The Snow." Reprinted by permission of Curtis Brown, Ltd. Copyright © 1960 by Donald Hall. First published in Fall, 1960, issue of *Partisan Review*.

The Devin-Adair Company. Patrick Kavanagh, "Father Mat," copyright 1964 by Patrick Kavanagh.

The Dolmen Press Limited. Austin Clarke, "Ancient Lights," from *Later Poems* (1961) and "Mnemosyne Lay in Dust" (Sections I, II, VI, and XVIII) from *Mnemosyne Lay in Dust* (1966). Thomas Kinsella, "A Country Walk," from *Downstream* (1962), and "First Light," from *Wormwood* (1966). John Montague, "The Trout" and "All Legendary Obstacles," from *All Legendary Obstacles* (1966). Reprinted by permission of The Dolmen Press Limited.

Doubleday & Company, Inc. "In All These Acts," copyright © 1962 by Brother Antoninus, from *The Hazards of Holiness* by Brother Antoninus. Reprinted by permission of Doubleday & Company, Inc. "Give Way, Ye Gates" and "Orchids," copyright 1948 by Theodore Roethke, from *The Collected Poems of Theodore Roethke*. Reprinted by permission of Doubleday & Company, Inc. "All of the Fruits Had Fallen," copyright © 1955 by Delmore Schwartz, from *Summer Knowledge* by Delmore Schwartz. Reprinted by permission of Doubleday & Company, Inc.

Dufour Editions. Permission to reprint poems by R. S. Thomas, Austin Clarke, and John Montague granted by Dufour Editions.

Faber and Faber Ltd. "Listen, Put on Morning" from *The White Threshold* (1949) by W. S. Graham, and "On the Move" from *The Sense of Movement* (1957) by Thom Gunn are reprinted by permission of Faber and Faber Ltd.

Farrar, Straus & Giroux, Inc. Reprinted by permission of Farrar, Straus & Giroux, Inc., John Berryman, "Dream Song 29" and "Dream Song 53" from *77 Dream Songs* by John Berryman © copyright 1959, 1962, 1963, 1964 by John Berryman. Robert Lowell, "Man and Wife" and "To Delmore Schwartz" from *Life Studies* by Robert Lowell © copyright by Robert Lowell 1958. Robert Lowell, "Water" and "Fall, 1961" from *For the Union Dead* © copyright by Robert Lowell 1962.

Ian Hamilton Finlay, "Orkney Interior," from *The Dancers Inherit the Party* (1962), reprinted by permission of the author.

Grove Press. "The Kingfishers" from *The Distances* by Charles Olson. Reprinted by permission of Grove Press, Inc. Copyright © 1950, 1951, 1953, 1960 by Charles Olson.

Ramon Guthrie, "Laura Age Eight," by permission of the author.

Harcourt, Brace & World, Inc. "The Thousand Things," from *Torse 3*, © 1962, by Christopher Middleton. Reprinted by permission of Harcourt, Brace & World,

Inc. "Advice to a Prophet," © 1959 by Richard Wilbur. Reprinted from his volume *Advice to a Prophet and Other Poems* by permission of Harcourt, Brace & World, Inc.

Harper & Row, Publishers. From *Lupercal* by Ted Hughes, "An Otter," Copyright © 1960 by Ted Hughes; "November," Copyright © 1960 by Ted Hughes; "Pike," Copyright © 1959 by Ted Hughes. From *Wodwo* by Ted Hughes, "Cadenza," Copyright © 1967 by Ted Hughes. From *Traveling Through the Dark* by William Stafford, "Elegy," Copyright © 1967 by William Stafford. From *Ariel* by Sylvia Plath, "Daddy," Copyright © 1963 by Ted Hughes; "Death & Co.," Copyright © 1963 by Ted Hughes; "Ariel," Copyright © 1965 by Ted Hughes. All reprinted by permission of Harper & Row, Publishers. "Romans Angry about the Inner World" from *The Light Around the Body* by Robert Bly. Copyright © 1967 by Robert Bly. Reprinted by permission of Harper & Row, Publishers.

Rupert Hart-Davis Limited. "Walter Llywarch" from *Tares* (1961). Reprinted by permission of Rupert Hart-Davis Limited, Publishers.

David Higham Associates, Ltd. D. J. Enright, "Apocalypse," from *Addictions* (1962), published by Chatto & Windus. Reprinted by permission of David Higham Associates, Ltd.

Holt, Rinehart and Winston, Inc. "The Tomb of Michael Collins," from *Selected Poems* by Denis Devlin. Copyright © 1956 by Marie C. Figarolo di Gropello. Reprinted by permission of Holt, Rinehart and Winston, Inc. "A Death," from *A Sense of the World* by Elizabeth Jennings. Copyright © 1958 by Elizabeth Jennings. Reprinted by permission of Holt, Rinehart and Winston, Inc.

Houghton Mifflin Company. Elizabeth Bishop, "Arrival at Santos" from *Poems North and South* (1955) published by the Houghton Mifflin Company. Anne Sexton, "You, Doctor Martin" from *To Bedlam and Part Way Back* (1960), and "The Starry Night" from *All My Pretty Ones* (1962), published by the Houghton Mifflin Company. Galway Kinnell, "Vapor Trail Reflected in the Frog Pond" from *Body Rags* (1967), published by Houghton Mifflin Company and reprinted with their permission.

Thomas Kinsella, "A Country Walk," "First Light," and "Ritual of Departure" reprinted by permission of the author.

Little, Brown and Company. Quotation from *The Autobiography of Bertrand Russell*. Copyright 1951, 1952, 1953, 1956, by Bertrand Russell. Copyright © 1961 by Allen and Unwin Ltd., Copyright © 1967 by George Allen and Unwin Ltd. By permission of Atlantic-Little, Brown and Company.

The Sterling Lord Agency. LeRoi Jones, "An Agony. As Now" from *The Dead Lecturer*, published 1964 by Grove Press. Copyright © 1964 by LeRoi Jones. Reprinted by permission of The Sterling Lord Agency.

The Macmillan Company. "British Leftish Poetry," "Reflections in a Slum," and "Old Wife in High Spirits," by Hugh MacDiarmid. Reprinted with permission of The Macmillan Company from *Collected Poems* by Hugh MacDiarmid. © Christopher Murray Grieve 1948, 1962. "On a Certain Engagement South of Seoul" by Hayden Carruth. Reprinted with permission of The Macmillan Company from *The Crow and the Heart* by Hayden Carruth. © Hayden Carruth

1959. "Poems of My Lambretta" by Paul Goodman. Reprinted with permission of The Macmillan Company from *The Lordly Hudson* by Paul Goodman. © Paul Goodman 1960. "The Clown, He Dances in the Clearing by Night" by Ramon Guthrie. Reprinted with permission of The Macmillan Company from *Graffiti* by Ramon Guthrie. © Ramon Guthrie 1959. "Waterlily Fire" by Muriel Rukeyser. Reprinted with permission of The Macmillan Company from *Waterlily Fire* by Muriel Rukeyser. © Muriel Rukeyser 1962. "Ruins for These Times" by Theodore Weiss. Reprinted with permission of The Macmillan Company from *The Medium* by Theodore Weiss. Copyright © Theodore Weiss 1959–1960, 1962–1965.

The Marvell Press. "No Road" and "Reasons for Attendance" by Philip Larkin are reprinted from *The Less Deceived* (1955) by permission of The Marvell Press, Hessle, Yorkshire, England.

John Montague, "The First Invasion of Ireland," from *Poisoned Lands and Other Poems* (1961), reprinted by permission of the author.

Richard Murphy, selections from "The Battle of Aughrim," by permission of the author.

Howard Nemerov, "The Mud Turtle," by permission of the author.

New Directions Publishing Corporation. "Away above a harborful" by Lawrence Ferlinghetti, *A Coney Island of the Mind*, © 1955 by Lawrence Ferlinghetti. Reprinted by permission of New Directions Publishing Corporation. "Losing Track" by Denise Levertov, *O Taste and See*, © 1963 by Denise Levertov Goodman. Reprinted by permission of New Directions Publishing Corporation. "Doubled Mirrors" by Kenneth Rexroth, *Collected Shorter Poems*, copyright 1952 by Kenneth Rexroth. Reprinted by permission of New Directions Publishing Corporation. "The Moebius Strip" by Charles Olson, *Selected Writings*, © 1960 by Charles Olson. Reprinted by permission of New Directions Publishing Corporation.

W. W. Norton & Company, Inc. "The Ancestors" from *Nonsequences: Selfpoems* (1965) by Christopher Middleton, reprinted by permission of W. W. Norton & Company, Inc. Copyright © 1961, 1962, 1963, 1964, 1965 by Christopher Middleton.

Harold Ober Associates. "Bell Buoy" from *The Drunk in the Furnace* (1960) by W. S. Merwin. Reprinted by permission of Harold Ober Associates. Copyright © 1957 by W. S. Merwin.

Oxford University Press. "Four Kantian Lyrics" from *A Peopled Landscape* by Charles Tomlinson. © Oxford University Press 1963. Reprinted by permission. "The Fox" from *American Scenes* by Charles Tomlinson. © Oxford University Press 1966. Reprinted by permission.

Random House, Inc. Alfred A. Knopf, Inc. "A Country Walk" by Thomas Kinsella. © Copyright 1962 by Thomas Kinsella. Reprinted from *Nightwalker and Other Poems* by Thomas Kinsella, by permission of Alfred A. Knopf, Inc. "First Light" by Thomas Kinsella. © Copyright 1966 by Thomas Kinsella, by permission of Alfred A. Knopf, Inc. Sections 6 and 7 from "Heart's Needle" by W. D. Snodgrass, from *Heart's Needle* by W. D. Snodgrass. © Copyright 1959 by W. D. Snodgrass. Reprinted by permission of Alfred A. Knopf, Inc. "Here" by Philip

Larkin, © Copyright 1964 by Philip Larkin. Reprinted from *The Whitsun Weddings*, by Philip Larkin, by permission of Random House, Inc.

Routledge & Kegan Paul Ltd. "Against Death" from *The Collector and Other Poems* (1959) and "Dismissal" from *At the White Monument* (1963) by Peter Redgrove. Reprinted by permission of Routledge & Kegan Paul Ltd.

Scorpion Press. "The Return" from *A Doomsday Book* (1965) and "Scissor-Man" from *The Broken Places* (1963) by George MacBeth. Reprinted by permission of the Scorpion Press.

Charles Scribner's Sons. The following poems are reprinted with the permission of Charles Scribner's Sons: "The Riddle" (Copyright 1957 Migrant Books) and "Kore" (Copyright © 1961 Robert Creeley) from *For Love* and "The Window" (Copyright © 1966 Robert Creeley) from *Words* by Robert Creeley; "After a Passage in Baudelaire," "Strains of Sight," and "Shelley's *Arethusa* Set to New Measures" from *Roots and Branches* by Robert Duncan (Copyright © 1964 Robert Duncan); and "Seeing the Frog" (Copyright © 1963 *Saturday Review*) from *To Mix with Time* (1963) by May Swenson.

The Swallow Press, Incorporated. "Death of a Cat" from *Public Dooms and Private Destinations* (1963) by James Schevill, reprinted by permission of The Swallow Press, Incorporated, Chicago.

University of Chicago Press. "In Santa Maria del Popolo," reprinted from *My Sad Captains* by Thom Gunn by permission of The University of Chicago Press. Copyright © 1961 by Thom Gunn.

Wesleyan University Press. The following poems are reprinted by permission of Wesleyan University Press: From Donald Davie, *Events and Wisdoms*, "Bolyai, the Geometer," copyright © 1965 by Donald Davie; and "After an Accident," copyright © 1965 by Donald Davie. From James Dickey, *Poems 1957–1967*, "The Firebombing," copyright © 1964 by James Dickey (this poem first appeared in *Poetry* magazine). From Louis Simpson, *A Dream of Governors*, "Carentan O Carentan" copyright © 1959 by Louis Simpson. From James Wright, *The Branch Will Not Break*, "A Blessing" copyright © 1961 by James Wright (this poem first appeared in *Poetry* magazine).

David Wright, "Meditation on Identity," by permission of the author.

For my daughter, Laura

FOREWORD

A NEW BODY OF POETRY has arisen in the United States, the United Kingdom, and Ireland since World War II, and this small anthology is intended to suggest its scope and to present some of its outstanding examples. New figures have emerged and begun to mature in the shadow of the old. A few have already achieved considerable stature and reputation, so much so that they are to be found in several recent anthologies that cover modern poetry since its beginnings. Thus, Robert Lowell, Randall Jarrell, Howard Nemerov, Philip Larkin, Charles Tomlinson, and Richard Wilbur are all represented in *Chief Modern Poets of England and America* (Fourth Edition), edited by Gerald D. Sanders, John H. Nelson, and myself. They now appear in this collection as well, though I have avoided any repetition of poems in the two books. I have also included three poets from a much older generation: Hugh MacDiarmid (born in 1892), Austin Clarke (1896), and Ramon Guthrie (1896). These vigorous writers are still hardly known in this country. Clarke is Irish, MacDiarmid is a Scotsman, and Guthrie, though very American, is part of the half-expatriate generation of the Great War and the twenties in Paris. But they have each experienced a poetic resurgence, or come into belated recognition, fairly recently. For example, Austin Clarke's masterpiece, *Mnemosyne Lay in Dust*, was published in 1966.

The vast majority of the poets included, though, have in every sense emerged only since the last war. Such interesting figures as Sylvia Plath, Ted Hughes, Thomas Kinsella, Charles Olson, Robert Duncan, Robert Creeley, Allen Ginsberg, and indeed most of the poets represented have come into their own since the last time people looked to see what was going on. In the past few years alone we have seen the appearance—among others—of such outstanding volumes of the period as Sylvia Plath's *Ariel*, Thomas Kinsella's *Wormwood*, and Robert Duncan's *Roots and Branches*. It is to be hoped that students will be helped by this collection to realize the continuing dynamism of our poetry in English and the unpredictable possibilities it holds for the future. Of course, a volume as small as this one can only sample the richness of the current poetic scene. For a more inclusive though still highly selective representation, the reader may wish to refer to my *The New Modern Poetry: British and American Poetry since World War II*, published earlier this year. Well over half the poems that follow, however, are not included in that anthology. Indeed, many were not yet available when it was ready for publication.

Like *Chief Modern Poets of England and America*, the present anthology is divided into a British and an American section. Within each section, the poets are arranged in order of birth; where there is more than one poem by a single author, the poems are arranged in order of publication. A brief biographical and bibliographical account of each poet appears at the back of the book.

M. L. R.

Suffern, N.Y.

Contents

100 POSTWAR POEMS

POETRY SINCE 1945

IN ONE SENSE, we find no very sharp breaks between the poetry of the three or four decades before World War II and that since 1945. As before, most of the more "extreme" efforts are American rather than English or Irish, though in fact that situation seems to be changing now. The poetic pursuit of the limits of sensibility under pressure, once the particular province of Pound, Eliot, and Hart Crane, has in our time been carried forward by the confessional poets especially —Robert Lowell, John Berryman, Sylvia Plath, and others. The formal experimentalism of Pound and Williams has been recognizably taken up by the Projectivist, or Black Mountain, poets—Charles Olson, Robert Duncan, Robert Creeley, and a few others. Surrealist imagery, imagistic compression, extensions of free verse techniques, the encouragement of colloquialism, the cultivation of extraordinary frankness—all these have well-known sources and inspiration in the poetry of the between-wars era, and even earlier.

Little by little, though, as one becomes familiar with the new poetry, certain differences make themselves clear. Underlying everything else, perhaps, are the frankness I have mentioned and with it a sense, admittedly not universal, of private despair, hopeless in the face of great impersonal, destructive, coarsening processes. In a work like Lowell's *Life Studies*, in the poems of Sylvia Plath's *Ariel*, in the many poems that circle round and round the themes of war and recent history on the one hand and of psychological distress on the other, and in those that resort to motifs and language at one time taboo but now widely familiar both in literature and in the conversation of educated young people, we are forced to recognize deeply altered emphases. So swift has been this development that the allowable vocabulary and avowable experience of generations no more than twenty years apart are far more unlike than at any time in the past. One must recognize that what William Dean Howells used to call "the larger latitude" (little dreaming what it would one day come to mean) is for a great

1

many people no longer shocking but the common staple of life and discourse, taken for granted as such.

No doubt the breakdown of traditional élite reticences and assumptions is involved in all this. The common experience is being assimilated into poetic awareness at an accelerated pace, and the alienation of the artist becomes a sharing—however symbolic merely—of the disaffection, humiliations, and needs of the deprived many. As Muriel Rukeyser writes in "Waterlily Fire": "Whatever can happen to anyone can happen to me." The main road to this sharing appears to be the confessional one. That is, the poet deliberately casts off the mask of impersonality, of a speaking self or *persona* different from his literal self, and speaks directly to his own condition: his actual, daily problems, his sexual experience, his psychological difficulties and triumphs. What would once have been well-kept family secrets, too humiliating to bear public allusion of even the most oblique sort, now become, often, the center of attention. The difference between Eliot and Lowell is instructive. Throughout Eliot's poetry one is aware of intimate psychological crises as somehow involved in the tone and tensions of the poetry, but there is never a personal note that actually gives the game away. Indeed, no poet has been as adept as Eliot at foiling those who would pry into his life. Lowell, on the other hand, has made his work the very embodiment of Whitman's warning that "whoever touches this touches a man"—far more than Whitman actually did. In addition to the confessional poets named in the first paragraph, one would have to add a number of others represented in this anthology who have tried to do something of the same kind: Allen Ginsberg, Paul Goodman, Theodore Roethke, Muriel Rukeyser, Anne Sexton, W. D. Snodgrass—these at least in the United States. In the British Isles we should at any rate have to include Austin Clarke, Donald Davie, Thomas Kinsella, John Montague, Peter Redgrove, though for most of them this has been a quite recent development and is even so by no means representative of their whole poetic character at any time.

There is a psychoanalytical dimension in the aesthetic principle behind confessional poetry. That is, it is felt that transcendence is to be gained through immersion in the anguish of facing up to one's actual nature and relationships. The depressive result (comparable to that following deep analysis) of letting the truth flood in on one from both within and without is a necessary prelude to the reorganizing of the self and of a consequent encompassment of the deepest issues or confrontations. Making oneself "available" to the outside world,

destroying the mystery of the Poet to reveal his full human vulner-
ability, is a function of that "sharing" of which I have spoken, and in
a sense of the democratization of the poetic art. Many, though not
all, of the confessional poets feel their own very specific experiences
as somehow embodiments of the national and even international
predicament and crisis. This identification derives from the same
kind of insight that Bertrand Russell describes in his *Autobiography*
as coming to him suddenly once when, after having been deeply
stirred by Gilbert Murray's reading aloud of his translation of *Hip-
polytus*, he discovered that the wife of his friend Alfred North White-
head was in terrible pain:

Ever since my marriage, my emotional life had been calm and superficial.
I had forgotten all the deeper issues, and had been content with flippant
cleverness. Suddenly the ground seemed to give way beneath me, and I
found myself in quite another region. Within five minutes I went through
some such reflections as the following: the loneliness of the human soul
is unendurable; nothing can penetrate it except the highest intensity of
the sort of love that religious teachers have preached; whatever does not
spring from this motive is harmful or, at best, useless; it follows that war
is wrong, that a public school education is abominable, that the use of
force is to be deprecated, and in human relations one should penetrate to
the core of loneliness in each person and speak to them. . . . At the end
of those five minutes, I had become a completely different person. For a
time, a sort of mystical illumination possessed me. I felt that I knew the
thought of everybody that I met in the streets, and though this was no
doubt an illusion, I did, in fact, find myself in far closer touch than pre-
viously with all my friends, and many of my acquaintances.

Russell's experience is comparable to the heroic and the tragic vision of such early modern poets of his own generation as Yeats, Pound,
Eliot, Williams, and Lawrence. (These poets were all born between
1865 and 1888, and Russell himself was born in 1871.) The letter of
Russell's just quoted suggests at once the remarkable power of art—
the Gilbert Murray reading—to reopen and redirect sensibility and,
partly by contrast, the basic orientation of our most serious poetry.
The chief difference between the revelation that came to Russell and
that of the poets had to do with the central realization of the soul's
loneliness, what Yeats called its "solitude." For Russell the realization
suggested a program of moral self-direction. The poets did not reject
such a program, but they were already saturated with the Romantic
motif of the alienated Self. The disillusionment with a society that
took war and repression and privilege for granted meant for them a

far more prolonged immersion in the desolate implications of existence and a varied search for the artistic means to encompass them.
They were much more involved, subjectively, with the new violence
emerging in their age, the intensified pressures on sensibility, the tech-
nological impact that makes human beings into manipulable masses,
and the destructive results of the process. The lessons of forerunners
like Coleridge in "Dejection: An Ode" and Keats in "Ode to a
Nightingale" took on new dimensions, as a clear result, and required
new formal inventions and more ruthless self-probing. The sense,
the *reality*, of psychic fragmentation required the cultivation of new
kinds of power, speed, hardness, and psychological dynamics, and new
devices for ordering poems as a result.

After the older modern generation I have named, the struggle to
maintain the forward thrust of a relatively violent, experimental,
inventive poetry fell mainly to the Americans, as I have already suggested. The process goes on, though less obviously, in the British Isles
as well, with an intensification, if not a drastic escalation, quite
recently. The renewed interest in Ezra Pound and in Continental
poetry, the quite new interest in William Carlos Williams and in
current international tendencies such as the Concrete movement, the
powerful impact of Sylvia Plath's *Ariel* and of the Beat poets, and the
new tendencies in Irish poetry are all matters of the 1960's. So also
is the influence of other genres—the drama of Harold Pinter and
others, the new fiction and even the new movements in jazz and
popular music. The atmosphere has changed a good deal even since
A. Alvarez wrote, in the preface to his anthology *The New Poetry*
(1962) that

sometime in the twenties Thomas Hardy remarked to Robert Graves that
"*vers libre* could come to nothing in England. All we can do is to write
on the old themes in the old styles, but try to do a little better than those
who went before us." Since about 1930, the machinery of modern English
poetry seems to have been controlled by a series of negative feedbacks
designed to produce exactly the effect Hardy wanted.

If the reader will turn to Philip Larkin's poems (pages 38–40),
he will find them brilliant illustrations of the best work of the type
Alvarez—England's foremost advocate of a new, "American" orientation—was criticizing. They will, by the same token perhaps, illustrate
the kind of basic problem that much English verse today presents to
an American. It suggests the stubborn resistance to a vision of possibility, in the art itself as well as in the perspectives of life, that marks

so much British writing. Larkin is tough-minded, colloquial, and "realistic" in a sense, say, that D. H. Lawrence, whose tone he echoes in an inverse way, would have hated. One can see in it just that admission of defeat against which Lawrence struggled so hard. Larkin's is a very slight turn on Lawrence, actually; but that turn means the shutting off of possibility through acceptance of what Lawrence and the whole revolutionary generation of early modern poets tried to destroy.

Despite Alvarez's castigation of it as "academic-administrative verse, polite, knowledgeable, efficient, polished, and, in its quiet way, even intelligent"—qualities he links with the "image of the postwar Welfare State Englishman"—the Larkin tone is unquestionably durable. Its wry wit and brilliant mimicry of the cliché-ridden mentality in which the speaker feels himself trapped are very close to expressing quite accurately something deep in the national psyche. So I do not think that the restraint of British poetry is at all likely to break down completely. When, a decade or so after the War, it seemed possible that delayed hysteria (after the wartime self-repressions), foreign influences, and the outbreak of emotionalism signaled by the early successes of Dylan Thomas might combine to work mighty change, Robert Conquest and the group called The Movement arose to hold the fort with a program of neoclassical law and order leavened by satirical wit. Conquest's anthology *New Lines* (1957), with its introductory manifesto, was presented as an exemplary collection and began a war of anthologies in which Alvarez's *The New Poetry* became its chief antagonist. Conquest's *New Lines 2* (1963) staunchly held the theoretical line in its introduction but not in the poems presented. Similarly, Donald Davie, at first one of the chief literary theorists of the movement, and certainly the most interesting, began drifting toward opposite positions in both his critical interests and his poetry. Another influential movement, called The Group, showed a similar, perhaps even more rapid evolution.

The work of Charles Tomlinson suggests one way in which English poetry is moving, however quietly, into a new strength. Tomlinson has studied French and American poetry, has lived in the United States—as a surprising number of the most interesting new English and Irish poets have—and is hardly less English for all of that except in the widened range of his ear and mind. He has not Larkin's humor and talent (shared with his friend Kingsley Amis) for catching fashionably hard-boiled speech and the dream banalities of fiction and film and working them into his art. But he has cultivated the power of losing himself in his literal materials and of letting their coloration, shape, and ambience engulf and direct him. He establishes, not so much a speaking personality commenting ironically and perhaps sadly on this or that subject, as a concrete discovery that comes into its own. In this mode of poetic thought, he seems clearly akin to such Projectivist American poets as Robert Creeley, Denise Levertov, and Charles Olson, all of whom have been preoccupied with the making of a poetry deeply engaged with the felt moment of existence. Very often, Tomlinson combines imagistic method with meditative exposition and avoids the direct interference of his own private personality. His stanzas usually have a regularity based on the number of lines but not on mechanical paralleling of line-lengths or rhythms. He works with great tact to use the result of his poetic studies with truth to his British materials and idiom.

We come closest to a British poetry of sheer power, however, in the work of Ted Hughes. During their relatively brief period together before her death, Hughes and his American wife, Sylvia Plath, each wrote a body of poems remarkable both in discipline and in explosive force and ferocity. Until quite recently, Hughes's writing was marked by unusual surface objectivity. He packed into a poem like "Pike" a great deal of the desperate emotion that other poets were expressing directly, in subjective outcries and through confessional means. The savagery of "Pike," however, is totally externalized. Whatever inward disturbance the poet feels, and however unstable and disastrous he may fear the total situation of England and of man to be, he transfers it all to the ravenous pike that he describes, to the anecdotes he tells, to the setting he recreates at the end of the poem. It is only in retrospect that we realize that we have been given archetypal horror and perhaps inner panic; we have been psychologically controlled in the way that some great primitive storyteller might have managed it, but with a modern sophistication manipulating us as well.

I have stressed a poetry of psychological pressure of various sorts because so much of the most telling work of the new age is in one sense or another of this order. Personal crisis and the theme of war are all too significantly and self-evidently pervasive motifs of our poets. It should be clear, however, that we still have poetry of tranquility, love, joy, and the more idiosyncratic interests of individual poets. Still, such motifs are never totally unrelated to the preoccupations of the age in which they appear, and neither are the purely formal concerns of any literary era. The extraordinary virtuosity and delight in poetic richness of Robert Duncan, for instance, or—with a more acid edge and other differences—of Christopher Middleton, are put to the service of those preoccupations in unique ways. I shall not press the point any further, however. Poetry interests us first of all as *itself*, poetry, a "prospect of delight" in its aesthetic aspect, however forbidding its subjects may often be. I have chosen these hundred poems as much with this thought in mind as with my plainer purpose of giving a fair sampling of the poetry of the United States and the British Isles since the last war.

The British Poets

HUGH MacDIARMID (CHRISTOPHER GRIEV

b. 1892

British Leftish Poetry, 1930–40

Auden, MacNeice, Day Lewis, I have read them all,
Hoping against hope to hear the authentic call.
"A tragical disappointment. There was I
Hoping to hear old Aeschylus, when the Herald
Called out, 'Theognis, bring your chorus forward.'
Imagine what my feelings must have been!
But then Dexitheus pleased me coming forward
And singing his Bœotian melody:
But next came Chaeris with his music truly
That turned me sick and killed me very nearly.
And never in my lifetime, man nor boy,
Was I so vexed as at the present moment;
To see the Pnyx, at this time of the morning,
Quite empty, when the Assembly should be full" *
And know the explanation I must pass is this
—You cannot light a match on a crumbling wall.

Reflections in a Slum

A lot of the old folk here—all that's left
Of them after a lifetime's infernal thrall
Remind me of a Bolshie the "whites" buried alive
Up to his nose, just able to breathe, that's all.

Watch them. You'll see what I mean. When found
His eyes had lost their former gay twinkle.
Ants had eaten *that* away; but there was still
Some life in him . . . his forehead *would* wrinkle!

And I remember Gide telling
Of Valéry and himself:

* Aristophanes, *The Acharnians*.

11

"It was a long time ago. We were young.
We had mingled with idlers
Who formed a circle
Round a troupe of wretched mountebanks.
It was on a raised strip of pavement
In the boulevard Saint Germain,
In front of the Statue of Broca.
They were admiring a poor woman,
Thin and gaunt, in pink tights, despite the cold.
Her team-mate had tied her, trussed her up,
Skilfully from head to foot,
With a rope that went round her
I don't know how many times,
And from which, by a sort of wriggling,
She was to manage to free herself.
Sorry image of the fate of the masses!
But no one thought of the symbol.
The audience merely contemplated
In stupid bliss the patient's efforts.
She twisted, she writhed, slowly freed one arm,
Then the other, and when at last
The final cord fell from her
Valéry took me by the arm:
'Let's go now! She has ceased suffering!' "

Oh, if only ceasing to suffer
They were able to become men.
Alas! how many owe their dignity,
Their claim on our sympathy,
Merely to their misfortune.
Likewise, so long as a plant has not blossomed
One can hope that its flowering will be beautiful.
What a mirage surrounds what has not yet blossomed!
What a disappointment when one can no longer
Blame the abjection on the deficiency!
It is good that the voice of the indigent,
Too long stifled, should manage
To make itself heard.
But I cannot consent to listen
To nothing but that voice.
Man does not cease to interest me

When he ceases to be miserable.
Quite the contrary!
That it is important to aid him
In the beginning goes without saying,
Like a plant it is essential
To water at first,
But this is in order to get it to flower
And I *am concerned with the blossom.*

Old Wife in High Spirits

In an Edinburgh Pub

An auld wumman cam' in, a mere rickle o' banes, in a faded
      black dress
And a bonnet wi' beads o' jet rattlin' on it;
A puir-lookin' cratur, you'd think she could haurdly ha'e had less
Life left in her and still lived, but dagonit!

He gied her a stiff whisky—she was nervous as a troot
And could haurdly haud the tumbler, puir cratur;
Syne he gied her anither, joked wi' her, and anither, and syne
Wild as the whisky up cam' her nature.

The rod that struck water frae the rock in the desert
Was naething to the life that sprang oot o' her;
The dowie auld soul was twinklin' and fizzin' wi' fire;
You never saw ocht sae souple and kir.

Like a sackful o' monkeys she was, and her lauchin'
Loupit up whiles to incredible heights;
Wi' ane owre the eight her temper changed and her tongue
Flew juist as the forkt lichtnin' skites.

The heich skeich auld cat was fair in her element;
Wanton as a whirlwind, and shairly better that way
Than a' crippen thegither wi' laneliness and cauld
Like a foretaste o' the graveyaird clay.

Some folk nae doot'll condemn gie'in' a guid spree
To the puir dune body and raither she endit her days

Like some auld tashed copy o' the Bible yin sees
On a street book-barrow's tipenny trays.

A' I ken is weel-fed and weel-put-on though they be
Ninety per cent o' respectable folk never hae
As muckle life in their creeshy carcases frae beginnin' to end
As kythed in that wild auld carline that day!

AUSTIN CLARKE *b.* 1896

Ancient Lights

When all of us wore smaller shoes
And knew the next world better than
The knots we broke, I used to hurry
On missions of my own to Capel
Street, Bolton Street and Granby Row
To see what man has made. But darkness
Was roomed with fears. Sleep, stripped by woes
I had been taught, beat door, leaped landing,
Lied down the bannisters of naught.

Being sent to penance, come Saturday,
I shuffled slower than my sins should.
My fears were candle-spiked at side-shrines,
Rays lengthened them in stained-glass. Confided
To night again, my grief bowed down,
Heard hand on shutter-knob. Did I
Take pleasure, when alone—how much—
In a bad thought, immodest look
Or worse, unnecessary touch?

Closeted in the confessional,
I put on flesh, so many years
Were added to my own, attempted
In vain to keep Dominican
As much i' the dark as I was, mixing

Whispered replies with his low words;
Then shuddered past the crucifix,
The feet so hammered, daubed-on blood-drip,
Black with lip-scrimmage of the damned.

Once as I crept from the church-steps,
Beside myself, the air opened
On purpose. Nature read in a flutter
An evening lesson above my head.
Atwirl beyond the leadings, corbels,
A cage-bird came among sparrows
(The moral inescapable)
Plucked, roof-mired, all in mad bits. O
The pizzicato of its wires!

Goodness of air can be proverbial:
That day, by the kerb at Rutland Square,
A bronze bird fabled out of trees,
Mailing the spearheads of the railings,
Sparrow at nails, I hailed the skies
To save the tiny dropper, found
Appetite gone. A child of clay
Has blustered it away. Pity
Could raise some littleness from dust.

What Sunday clothes can change us now
Or humble orders in black and white?
Stinking with centuries the act
Of thought. So think, man, as Augustine
Did, dread the ink-bespattered ex-monk,
And keep your name. No, let me abandon
Night's jakes. Self-persecuted of late
Among the hatreds of rent Europe,
Poetry burns at a different stake.

Still, still I remember aweful downpour
Cabbing Mountjoy Street, spun loneliness
Veiling almost the Protestant church,
Two backyards from my very home.
I dared to shelter at locked door.
There, walled by heresy, my fears
Were solved. I had absolved myself:

Feast-day effulgence, as though I gained
For life a plenary indulgence.

The sun came out, new smoke flew up,
The gutters of the Black Church rang
With services. Waste water mocked
The ballcocks: down-pipes sparrowing,
And all around the spires of Dublin
Such swallowing in the air, such cowling
To keep high offices pure: I heard,
From shore to shore, the iron gratings
Take half our heavens with a roar.

FROM *Mnemosyne Lay in Dust*

I

Past the house where he was got
In darkness, terrace, provision shop,
Wing-hidden convent opposite,
Past public-houses at lighting-up
Time, crowds outside them—Maurice Devane
Watched from the taxi window in vain
National stir and gaiety
Beyond himself: St. Patrick's Day,
The spike-ends of the Blue Coat school,
Georgian houses, ribald gloom
Rag-shadowed by gaslight, quiet pavements
      Moon-waiting in Blackhall Place.

For six weeks Maurice had not slept,
Hours pillowed him from right to left side,
Unconsciousness became the pit
Of terror. Void would draw his spirit,
Unself him. Sometimes he fancied that music,
Soft lights in Surrey, Kent, could cure him,
Hypnotic touch, until, one evening,
The death-chill seemed to mount from feet
To shin, to thigh. Life burning in groin
And prostate ached for a distant joy.

But nerves need solitary confinement.
    Terror repeals the mind.

Cabs ranked at Kingsbridge Station, Guinness
Tugs moored at their wooden quay, glinting
Of Liffey mudbank; hidden vats
Brewing intoxication, potstill,
Laddering of distilleries
Ready to sell their jollities,
Delirium tremens. Dublin swayed,
Drenching, drowning the shamrock: unsaintly
Mirth. The high departments were filed,
Yard, store, unlit. Whiskey-all-round,
Beyond the wealth of that square mile,
    Was healthing every round.

The eighteenth century hospital
Established by the tears of Madam
Steevens, who gave birth, people said, to
A monster with a pig's snout, pot-head.
The Ford turned right, slowed down. Gates opened,
Closed with a clang; acetylene glow
Of headlights. How could Maurice Devane
Suspect from weeping-stone, porch, vane,
The classical rustle of the harpies,
Hopping in filth among the trees,
The Mansion of Forgetfulness
    Swift gave us for a jest?

II

Straight-jacketing sprang to every lock
And bolt, shadowy figures shocked,
Wall, ceiling; hat, coat, trousers flung
From him, vest, woollens, Maurice was plunged
Into a steaming bath; half suffocated,
He sank, his assailants gesticulating,
A Keystone reel gone crazier;
The terror-peeling celluloid,
Whirling the figures into vapour,
    Dissolved them. All was void.

Drugged in the dark, delirious,
In vision Maurice saw, heard, struggle
Of men and women, shouting, groans.
In an accident at Westland Row,
Two locomotives with mangle of wheel-spokes,
Colliding: up-scatter of smoke, steel,
Above: the gong of ambulances.
Below, the quietly boiling hiss
Of steam, the winter-sleet of glances,
    The quiet boiling of pistons.

The crowds were noisy. Sudden cries
Of "Murder! Murder!" from a byeway,
The shriek of women with upswollen
Bodies, held down in torment, rolling
And giving birth to foundlings, shriek
After shriek, the blanket lifting unspeakable
Protrusions. The crowds were stumbling backward,
Barefooted cry of "Murder" scurried.
Police batoned eyesight into blackness.
    Bandages were blurred.

Maurice had wakened up. He saw a
Circular peep-hole rimmed with polished
Brass within the door. It gloomed.
A face was glaring into the bed-room
With bulging eyes and fierce moustache.
Quicker than thought, a torchlight flashed
From wall to pillow. Motionless,
It spied until the face had gone.
The sound of sleepers in unrest:
    Still watchful, the peep-hole shone.

What night was it, he heard the creaking
Of boots and tiptoed to the peep-hole?
Four men were carrying a coffin
Upon their shoulders. As they shuffled,
Far in his mind a hollaloo
Echoed: "The Canon of Killaloe . . ."
Death-chill would mount from feet to limbs,
His loins, secretion no longer burn.

Those shoulderers would come for him with
    The shroud, spade, last thud.

Nightly he watched a masquerade
Go by his cell and was afraid
Of one—the stooping, bald-headed madman
Who muttered curse after curse, his hands
Busily knitting, twiddling white reeds:
So huge, he seemed to be the leader.
The others tormented by their folly,
The narrows of the moon, crowded
Together, gibboned his gestures, followed
    That madman knitting reed, brow.

Once, getting out of bed, he peeped
Into the dormitory. Sheet
And slip were laundry-white. Dazes
Of electric light came down. Patients
Stirred fitfully. Their fidgetting marred
With scrawls the whiteness of the ward,
Gift of the moon. He wondered who
He was, but memory had hidden
All. Someone sat beside him, drew
    Chair nearer, murmured: "Think!"

One afternoon, he looked in dread
Into the ward outside. The beds
Were empty. Quiet sunshine glowed
On waxed floor and brass. He hurried
Across to the high window, stood
On the hot pipes to see the view.
Below there was a widespread garden,
With shrubberies, walks, summerhouses.
He stared in wonder from his bars,
    Saddened by the boughs.

VI

One night he heard heart-breaking sound.
It was a sigh unworlding its sorrow.
Another followed. Slowly he counted
Four different sighs, one after another.

"My mother," he anguished, "and my sisters
Have passed away. I am alone, now,
Lost in myself in a mysterious
Darkness, the victim in a story."
Far whistle of a train, the voice of steam.
Evil was peering through the peep-hole.

Suddenly heart began to beat
Too quickly, too loudly. It clamoured
As if it were stopping. He left the heat
And stumbled forward, hammered
The door, called out that he was dying.
Key turned. Body was picked up, carried
Beyond the ward, the bedwhite row
Of faces, into a private darkness.
Lock turned. He cried out. All was still.
He stood, limbs shivering in the chill.

He tumbled into half the truth:
Burial alive. His breath was shouting:
"Let, let me out." But words were puny.
Fists hushed on a wall of inward-outness.
Knees crept along a floor that stirred
As softly. All was the same chill.
He knew the wall was circular
And air was catchcry in the stillness
For reason had returned to tell him
That he was in a padded cell.

The key had turned again. Blankets
Were flung into blackness as if to mock
The cringer on the floor. He wrapped
The bedclothes around his limbs, shocked back
To sanity. Lo! in memory yet,
Margaret came in a frail night-dress,
Feet bare, her heavy plaits let down
Between her knees, his pale protectress.
Nightly restraint, unwanted semen
Had ended their romantic dream.

Early next morning, he awakened,
Saw only greyness shining down

From a skylight on the grey walls
Of leather, knew, in anguish, his bowels
Had opened. He turned, shivering, all shent.
Wrapping himself in the filthied blankets,
Fearful of dire punishment,
He waited there until a blankness
Enveloped him . . . When he raised his head up,
Noon-light was gentle in the bedroom.

XVIII

Rememorised, Maurice Devane
Went out, his future in every vein,
The Gate had opened. Down Steeven's Lane
The high wall of the Garden, to right
Of him, the Fountain with a horse-trough,
Illusions had become a story.
There was the departmental storey
Of Guinness's, God-given right
Of goodness in every barrel, tun,
They averaged. Upon that site
Of shares and dividends in sight
Of Watling Street and the Cornmarket,
At Number One in Thomas Street
Shone in the days of the ballad-sheet,
The house in which his mother was born.

PATRICK KAVANAGH 1905–1967

Father Mat

I

In a meadow
Beside the chapel three boys were playing football.
At the forge door an old man was leaning
Viewing a hunter-hoe. A man could hear
If he listened to the breeze the fall of wings—
How wistfully the sin-birds come home!

It was Confession Saturday, the first
Saturday in May; the May Devotions
Were spread like leaves to quieten
The excited armies of conscience.
The knife of penance fell so like a blade
Of grass that no one was afraid.

Father Mat came slowly walking, stopping to
Stare through gaps at ancient Ireland sweeping
In again with all its unbaptized beauty:
The calm evening,
The whitethorn blossoms,
The smell from ditches that were not Christian.
The dancer that dances in the hearts of men cried:
Look! I have shown this to you before—
The rags of living surprised
The joy in things you cannot forget.

His heavy hat was square upon his head,
Like a Christian Brother's;
His eyes were an old man's watery eyes,
Out of his flat nose grew spiky hairs.
He was a part of the place,
Natural as a round stone in a grass field;
He could walk through a cattle fair
And the people would only notice his odd spirit there.

His curate passed on a bicycle—
He had the haughty intellectual look
Of the man who never reads in brook or book;
A man designed
To wear a mitre,
To sit on committees—
For will grows strongest in the emptiest mind.

The old priest saw him pass
And, seeing, saw
Himself a mediaeval ghost.
Ahead of him went Power,
One who was not afraid when the sun opened a flower,
Who was never astonished

At a stick carried down a stream
Or at the undying difference in the corner of a field.

II

The Holy Ghost descends
At random like the muse
On wise man and fool,
And why should poet in the twilight choose?

Within the dim chapel was the grey
Mumble of prayer
To the Queen of May—
The Virgin Mary with the schoolgirl air.

Two guttering candles on a brass shrine
Raised upon the wall
Monsters of despair
To terrify deep into the soul.

Through the open door the hum of rosaries
Came out and blended with the homing bees.
           The trees
Heard nothing stranger than the rain or the wind
Or the birds—
But deep in their roots they knew a seed had sinned.

In the graveyard a goat was nibbling at a yew,
The cobbler's chickens with anxious looks
Were straggling home through nettles, over graves.
A young girl down a hill was driving cows
To a corner at the gable-end of a roofless house.

Cows were milked earlier,
The supper hurried,
Hens shut in,
Horses unyoked,
And three men shaving before the same mirror.

III

The trip of iron tips on tile
Hesitated up the middle aisle,

Heads that were bowed glanced up to see
Who could this last arrival be.

Murmur of women's voices from the porch,
Memories of relations in the graveyard.
On the stem
Of memory imaginations blossom.

            In the dim
Corners in the side seats faces gather,
Lit up now and then by a guttering candle
And the ghost of day at the window.
A secret lover is saying
Three Hail Marys that she who knows
The ways of women will bring
Cathleen O'Hara (he names her) home to him.
Ironic fate! Cathleen herself is saying
Three Hail Marys to her who knows
The ways of men to bring
Somebody else home to her—
"O may he love me."
What is the Virgin Mary now to do?

            IV

        From a confessional
The voice of Father Mat's absolving
Rises and falls like a briar in the breeze.
As the sins pour in the old priest is thinking
His fields of fresh grass, his horses, his cows,
His earth into the fires of Purgatory.
It cools his mind.
"They confess to the fields," he mused,
"They confess to the fields and the air and the sky,"
And forgiveness was the soft grass of his meadow by the river;
His thoughts were walking through it now.

His human lips talked on:
"My son,
Only the poor in spirit shall wear the crown;
Those down

Can creep in the low door
On to heaven's floor."

The Tempter had another answer ready:
"Ah lad, upon the road of life
'Tis best to dance with Chance's wife
And let the rains that come in time
Erase the footprints of the crime."

The dancer that dances in the hearts of men
Tempted him again:
"Look! I have shown you this before;
From this mountain-top I have tempted Christ
With what you see now
Of beauty—all that's music, poetry, art
In things you can touch every day.
I broke away
And rule all dominions that are rare;
I took with me all the answers to every prayer
That young men and girls pray for: love, happiness, riches—"
O Tempter! O Tempter!

V

As Father Mat walked home
Venus was in the western sky
And there were voices in the hedges:
"God the Gay is not the Wise."

"Take your choice, take your choice,"
Called the breeze through the bridge's eye.
"The domestic Virgin and Her Child
Or Venus with her ecstasy."

DENIS DEVLIN 1908–1959

The Tomb of Michael Collins

to Ignazio Silone

Much I remember of the death of men,
But his I most remember, most of all,
More than the familiar and forgetful
Ghosts who leave our memory too soon—
Oh, what voracious fathers bore him down!

It was all sky and heather, wet and rock,
No one was there but larks and stiff-legged hares
And flowers bloodstained. Then, Oh, our shame was so massive
Only a God embraced it and the angel
Whose hurt and misty rifle shot him down.

One by one the enemy dies off;
As the sun grows old, the dead increase,
We love the more the further from we're born!
The bullet found him where the bullet ceased,
And Gael and Gall went inconspicuous down.

II

There are the Four Green Fields we loved in boyhood,
There are some reasons it's no loss to die for:
Even it's no loss to die for having lived;
It is inside our life the angel happens
Life, the gift that God accepts or not,

Which Michael took with hand, with harsh, grey eyes,
He was loved by women and by men,
He fought a week of Sundays and by night
He asked what happened and he knew what was—
O Lord! how right that them you love die young!

He's what I was when by the chiming river
Two loyal children long ago embraced—
But what I was is one thing, what remember
Another thing, how memory becomes knowledge—
Most I remember him, how man is courage.

And sad, Oh sad, that glen with one thin stream
He met his death in; and a farmer told me
There was but one small bird to shoot: it sang
"Better Beast and know your end, and die
Than Man with murderous angels in his head."

III

I tell these tales—I was twelve years old that time.
Those of the past were heroes in my mind:
Edward the Bruce whose brother Robert made him
Of Ireland, King; Wolfe Tone and Silken Thomas
And Prince Red Hugh O'Donnell most of all.

The newsboys knew and the apple and orange women
Where was his shifty lodging Tuesday night;
No one betrayed him to the foreigner,
No Protestant or Catholic broke and ran
But murmured in their heart: here was a man!

Then came that mortal day he lost and laughed at,
He knew it as he left the armored car;
The sky held in its rain and kept its breath;
Over the Liffey and the Lee, the gulls,
They told his fortune which he knew, his death.

Walking to Vespers in my Jesuit school,
The sky was come and gone; "O Captain, my Captain!"
Walt Whitman was the lesson that afternoon—
How sometimes death magnifies him who dies,
And some, though mortal, have achieved their race.

NORMAN MacCAIG *b.* 1910

Innocence

What answer could she give
To the leopard in the dark?
To the clawed flower? to the dappled, twitching grass?
Only her own desire in which to live
Where anything might pass
And leave, such was its radiance, no mark.

The words that wounded her
Became part of her speech.
The face she feared looked through her gentle eyes;
And when she moved, midnight began to stir.
A world of muffled cries
Became the only world that she could reach.

She thought that radiance dead—
She who could not be seen,
Invisible in its brightness, now she was
Part of what it shone on. She drooped her head
And, soft as a leopard's paws,
Moused in the dark for what she once had been.

Near Midnight

I hear a bull blaring
From the sad shores of love.

Owls never haunt
The dark rides of this darkness,
So the one now calling over
The hayfield has the voice
Of a prophet returned
From the wilderness.

What wilderness shall I
Go into so that you will listen
When I return?

Under the few stars
Terns are dipping through the air
Towards the green islet
They rest on, quarrel on.
Though they seem half
Reptile, half angel, they
Are closer to me
Than you.
Their silence frightens me
Less than yours. —I listen,
I listen, and hear only
Reeds whispering their language and
A bull—sailor on shore
Calling the sirens in.
And all this
Is wilderness enough
For me.

R. S. THOMAS *b.* 1913

Walter Llywarch

I am, as you know, Walter Llywarch,
Born in Wales of approved parents,
Well goitred, round in the bum,
Sure prey of the slow virus
Bred in quarries of grey rain.

Born in autumn at the right time
For hearing stories from the cracked lips
Of old folk dreaming of summer,
I piled them on to the bare hearth
Of my own fancy to make a blaze
To warm myself, but achieved only

The smoke's acid that brings the smart
Of false tears into the eyes.

Months of fog, months of drizzle;
Thought wrapped in the grey cocoon
Of race, of place, awaiting the sun's
Coming, but when the sun came,
Touching the hills with a hot hand,
Wings were spread only to fly
Round and round in a cramped cage
Or beat in vain at the sky's window.

School in the week, on Sunday chapel:
Tales of a land fairer than this
Were not so tall, for others had proved it
Without the grave's passport, they sent
The fruit home for ourselves to taste.

Walter Llywarch—the words were a name
On a lost letter that never came
For one who waited in the long queue
Of life that wound through a Welsh valley.
I took instead, as others had done
Before, a wife from the back pews
In chapel, rather to share the rain
Of winter evenings, than to intrude
On her pale body; and yet we lay
For warmth together and laughed to hear
Each new child's cry of despair.

W. S. GRAHAM *b.* 1917

Listen. Put on Morning

Listen. Put on morning.
Waken into falling light.
A man's imagining
Suddenly may inherit

The handclapping centuries
Of his one minute on earth.
And hear the virgin juries
Talk with his own breath
To the corner boys of his street.
And hear the Black Maria
Searching the town at night.
And hear the playropes caa
The sister Mary in.
And hear Willie and Davie
Among bracken of Narnain
Sing in a mist heavy
With myrtle and listeners.
And hear the higher town
Weep a petition of fears
At the poorhouse close upon
The public heartbeat.
And hear the children tig
And run with my own feet
Into the netting drag
Of a suiciding principle.
Listen. Put on lightbreak.
Waken into miracle.
The audience lies awake
Under the tenements
Under the sugar docks
Under the printed moments.
The centuries turn their locks
And open under the hill
Their inherited books and doors
All gathered to distil
Like happy berry pickers
One voice to talk to us.
Yes listen. It carries away
The second and the years
Till the heart's in a jacket of snow
And the head's in a helmet white
And the song sleeps to be wakened
By the morning ear bright.
Listen. Put on morning.
Waken into falling light.

D. J. ENRIGHT *b.* 1920

Apocalypse

> After the New Apocalypse, very few members were still in posses-
> sion of their instruments. Hardly a musician could call a decent
> suit his own. Yet by the early summer of 1945, strains of sweet
> music floated on the air again. While the town still reeked of
> smoke, charred buildings and the stench of corpses, the Philhar-
> monic Orchestra bestowed the everlasting and imperishable joy
> which music never fails to give.
> —*from* The Muses on the Banks of the Spree,
> *a Berlin tourist brochure*

It soothes the savage doubts.
One Bach outweighs ten Belsens. If 200,000 people
Were remaindered at Hiroshima, the sales of So-and-So's
New novel reached a higher figure in as short a time.
So, imperishable paintings reappeared:
Texts were reprinted:
Public buildings reconstructed:
Human beings reproduced.

After the Newer Apocalypse, very few members
Were still in possession of their instruments
(Very few were still in possession of their members),
And their suits were chiefly indecent.
Yet, while the town still reeked of smoke, etc.,
The Philharmonic Trio bestowed, etc.

A civilization vindicated,
A race with three legs still to stand on!
True, the violin was shortly silenced by leukaemia,
And the pianoforte crumbled softly into dust.
But the flute was left. And one is enough.
All, in a sense, goes on. All is in order.

And the ten-tongued mammoth larks,
The forty-foot crickets and the elephantine frogs

Decided that the little chap was harmless,
At least he made no noise, on the banks of whatever river
    it used to be.

One day, a reed-warbler stepped on him by accident.
However, all, in a sense, goes on. Still the everlasting and
    imperishable joy
Which music never fails to give is being given.

DAVID WRIGHT *b.* 1920

Meditation on Identity

Arrangements of molecules held together by
Reactions of laws and forces
Have produced and have preserved this identity—

That is, what remembers, acts, is acted on, fears,
And being moved by, endorses
What it is part of: earth's, air's, and water's

Creation by that hypostasis up in the sky
Or whatever wherever houses
The imagination of the illusory.

Ephemeral substance of the body! Even
Its bone is transient, changes;
What rag is left of flesh the womb first clad us in?

Creation's matter flows through us like a river.
We have the loan of it, nothing's ours.
Man, plant, animal, everyone a borrower.

This one can understand, but not what makes up "I"
As a fountain rehearses
Water, to wield a shape from volatility.

DONALD DAVIE *b.* 1922

Bolyai, The Geometer

Arthur Allen, when he lived
In rooms beneath my rooms in Trinity,
Thought he had made a breakthrough that would turn
Mathematics inside out again,

As once geometry was spun around
Because the non-Euclidean emerged
Not out of nature, out of nothing extant
But simply as imaginable. Shade,

A flap of blackness folded back upon
Pillar and pediment that afternoon
Encroached upon the chapel portico
And there a wing whirled, flashing. So, I thought,

This turning inside-out is not so hard:
One looks across Front Square and there it is,
A wing that whirls white undersides, sustained
By what endangers it, the press of air.

And though his torque was different, not in nature,
And though my science is as pure as his,
Knowing no revolution more profound
Than that from black on white to white on black

(As though a shutter shot across the mind
One sees the lately formless as most formal,
The stanza most a unit when
Open at both ends, all transition) still

How pure is mathematics? Not enough
For Farkas Bolyai: "Not geometry
Is altogether pure. This is a wound
Large and perpetual upon my soul."

So with poetics: never a revolution
But has its mould. Look, in the overturning
Approaching comber, rolling inside out,
A roof of cream moves back through a mounting wall.

After An Accident

I

Smashed, and brought up against
Last things like pines'
Steep shadows and the purple
Hole in my darling's head,

I recall as an amulet
Against my shallowness
Uncalculated kindness
So much! Death, in my dream,

Half-length as in a portrait,
Cocks his eye, leads mine
Up a toothbrush ridge of pines
With an amused complicity

At seeing what is so
Beneath us as a mountain
Tower above us when
We have run out of road.

Death is about my age,
Smiling and dark, clean-shaven.
Behind him the valley-floor
Is ledged in a purple light.

Had I not sought the shade
Of what is so
Beneath us as chagrin,
I had not been afraid

Of his mountainous purple light,
Nor should I have run out
Of the soul of gratitude
Before I ran out of death.

II. BETWEEN DEAD AND ALIVE

For you to be thinking how
It was no bad place to lie in,
In this there was nothing morbid;
Nor was it too composed
In me, to thing of your dying
As of an emigration.

This century one in five
On that hillside has emigrated,
And this is not melancholy,
Nor the spaciousness disconcerting:
Between the dead and alive
The ratio there is a just one.

And yet I would have sworn
Such thoughts as these were tricks
Of tearful literature;
That thoughts so unresentful
As mine were could not mix
With terror and compunction.

III. THE HEARTLAND

And so it is clear that this
Heartland has to be painted
In unrepresentative colours;

That the forests under the mountains
Live in an orange light
Without reference to sunset.

How clear it is, and how
Incapable of being
Foreseen or offered as solace,

That remorse without regret

Is a possible state of the soul,
Like grief without resentment.

IV. WINDFALL

So Death is what one day
You have run out of, like
Luck or a bank-balance.
In that case, what is
Coming into it like?

Like coming into money!
The death we run out of is
Not the life we run out of;
The death that we may
With luck come into, is.

And without money, life
Is not worth living.
How did you manage
All these years,
Living and not living?

V. THANKS

You never did so much
As when you nearly died;
As if you nearly died
That I might show I lived.

That was no more your motive
Than it could have been my choice.
You cannot think I live
Just to give voice!

It was no poet's need you met,
And now survive,
But the need I had as a man
To know myself alive.

You never did so much
As when you nearly died;
You had to nearly die
For me to know I lived.

PHILIP LARKIN *b*. 1922

No Road

Since we agreed to let the road between us
Fall to disuse,
And bricked our gates up, planted trees to screen us,
And turned all time's eroding agents loose,
Silence, and space, and strangers—our neglect
Has not had much effect.

Leaves drift unswept, perhaps; grass creeps unmown;
No other change.
So clear it stands, so little overgrown,
Walking that way tonight would not seem strange,
And still would be allowed. A little longer,
And time will be the stronger,

Drafting a world where no such road will run
From you to me;
To watch that world come up like a cold sun,
Rewarding others, is my liberty.
Not to prevent it is my will's fulfilment.
Willing it, my ailment.

Reasons for Attendance

The trumpet's voice, loud and authoritative,
Draws me for a moment to the lighted glass
To watch the dancers—all under twenty-five—
Shifting intently, face to flushed face,
Solemnly on the beat of happiness.

—Or so I fancy, sensing the smoke and sweat,
The wonderful feel of girls. Why be out here?
But then, why be in there? Sex, yes, but what
Is sex? Surely, to think the lion's share
Of happiness is found by couples—sheer

Inaccuracy, as far as I'm concerned.
What calls me is that lifted, rough-tongued bell
(Art, if you like) whose individual sound
Insists I too am individual.
It speaks; I hear; others may hear as well,

But not for me, nor I for them; and so
With happiness. Therefore I stay outside,
Believing this; and they maul to and fro,
Believing that; and both are satisfied,
If no one has misjudged himself. Or lied.

Here

Swerving east, from rich industrial shadows
And traffic all night north; swerving through fields
Too thin and thistled to be called meadows,
And now and then a harsh-named halt, that shields
Workmen at dawn; swerving to solitude
Of skies and scarecrows, haystacks, hares and pheasants,
And the widening river's slow presence,
The piled gold clouds, the shining gull-marked mud,

Gathers to the surprise of a large town:
Here domes and statues, spires and cranes cluster
Beside grain-scattered streets, barge-crowded water,
And residents from raw estates, brought down
The dead straight miles by stealing flat-faced trolleys,
Push through plate-glass swing doors to their desires—
Cheap suits, red kitchen-ware, sharp shoes, iced lollies,
Electric mixers, toasters, washers, driers—

A cut-price crowd, urban yet simple, swelling
Where only salesmen and relations come
Within a terminate and fishy-smelling
Pastoral of ships up streets, the slave museum,
Tattoo-shops, consulates, grim head-scarfed wives;
And out beyond its mortgaged half-built edges
Fast-shadowed wheat-fields, running high as hedges,
Isolate villages, where removed lives

Loneliness clarifies. Here silence stands
Like heat. Here leaves unnoticed thicken,
Hidden weeds flower, neglected waters quicken,
Luminously-peopled air ascends;
And past the poppies bluish neutral distance
Ends the land suddenly beyond a beach
Of shapes and shingle. Here is unfenced existence:
Facing the sun, untalkative, out of reach.

DANNIE ABSE *b.* 1923

After the Release of Ezra Pound

In Jerusalem I asked
the ancient Hebrew poets to forgive you,
and what would Walt Whitman have said
and Thomas Jefferson?

—PAUL POTTS

In Soho's square mile of unoriginal sin
where the fraudulent neon lights haunt,
but cannot hide, the dinginess of vice,
the jeans and sweater boys spoke of Pound,
and you, Paul, repeated your question.

The chee-chee bums in Torino's laughed and
the virgins of St. Martin's School of Art.
The corner spivs with their Maltese masks
loitered for the two o'clock result,
and those in the restaurants of Greek Street
eating income tax did not hear the laugh.

Gentle Gentile, you asked the question.
Free now (and we praise this) Pound could answer.

The strip lighting of Soho did not fuse,
no blood trickled from a certain book
down the immaculate shelves of Zwemmer's.

But the circumcized did not laugh.
The swart nudes in the backrooms put on clothes
and the doors of the French pub closed.

Pound did not hear the raw Jewish cry,
the populations committed to the dark
when he muttered through microphones
of murderers. He, not I, must answer.

Because of the structures of a beautiful poet
you ask the man who is less than beautiful,
and wait in the public neurosis of Soho,
in the liberty of loneliness for an answer.

In the beer and espresso bars they talked
of Ezra Pound, excusing the silences of an old man,
saying there is so little time between
the parquet floors of an institution
and the boredom of the final box.

Why, Paul, if that ticking distance between
was merely a journey long enough
to walk the circumference of a Belsen,
Walt Whitman would have been eloquent,
and Thomas Jefferson would have cursed.

MICHAEL HAMBURGER *b.* 1924

Security

1

So he's got there at last, been received as a partner—
In a firm going bankrupt;
Found the right place (walled garden), arranged for a mortgage—
But they're pulling the house down
To make room for traffic.

Worse winds are rising. He takes out new policies
For his furniture, for his life,
At a higher premium
Against more limited risks.

2

Who can face the winds, till the panes crack in their frames?
And if a man faced them, what in the end could he do
But look for shelter like all the rest?
The winds too are afraid, and blow from fear.

3

I hear my children at play
And recall that one branch of the elm-tree looks dead;
Also that twenty years ago now I could have been parchment
Cured and stretched for a lampshade,
Who now have children, a lampshade
And the fear of those winds.

I saw off the elm-tree branch
To find that the wood was sound;
Mend the fences yet again,
Knowing they'll keep out no one,
Let alone the winds.
For still my children play,
And shall tomorrow, if the weather holds.

Homage to the Weather

A tide, high tide of golden air.

Where, till this moment, were the bees?
And when no hum made for the honeysuckle,
Fumbled,
Became a body,
Clung and drank,
Spindrift, disowned, the petals hung,
And wait, let go was what the summer meant.

A corner of the garden, ivy on broken slats,

A branch with orange puffs: buddleia globosa.
Between two gusts a flood of golden air,
Mere hush, perhaps, abeyance—but the bees
Clinging and drinking.

Walls they brought with them: black courtyard in Paris,
A bit of marble, tumbled, dust on leaves,
A goldfish pond, the traffic not remote,
Audible, yet excluded;
Flowering tree or shrub in any weathered city,
Walls to contain a quietness, a quiver,
Fulfilment of the year, bees to be stilled.

Between two gusts, cold waves, the golden tide.

IAN HAMILTON FINLAY *b.* 1925

Orkney Interior

Doing what the moon says, he shifts his chair
Closer to the stove and stokes it up
With the very best fuel, a mixture of dried fish
And tobacco he keeps in a bucket with crabs

Too small to eat. One raises its pincer
As if to seize hold of the crescent moon
On the calendar which is almost like a zodiac
With inexplicable and pallid blanks. Meanwhile

A lobster is crawling towards the clever
Bait that is set inside the clock
On the shelf by the wireless—and inherited dried fish
Soaked in whiskey and carefully trimmed

With potato flowers from the Golden Wonders
The old man grows inside his ears.
Click! goes the clock-lid, and the unfortunate lobster
Finds itself a prisoner inside the clock,

An adapted cuckoo-clock. It shows no hours, only
Tides and moons and is fitted out
With two little saucers, one of salt and one of water
For the lobster to live on while, each quarter-tide,

It must stick its head through the tiny trapdoor
Meant for the cuckoo. It will be trained to read
The broken barometer and wave its whiskers
To Scottish Dance Music, till it grows too old.

Then the old man will have to catch himself another lobster.
Meanwhile he is happy and takes the clock
Down to the sea. He stands and oils it
In a little rock pool that reflects the moon.

ELIZABETH JENNINGS *b.* 1926

A Death

"His face shone" she said,
"Three days I had him in my house,
Three days before they took him from his bed,
And never have I felt so close."

"Always alive he was
A little drawn away from me.
Looks are opaque when living and his face
Seemed hiding something, carefully."

"But those three days before
They took his body out, I used to go
And talk to him. That shining from him bore
No secrets. Living, he never looked or answered so."

Sceptic I listened, then
Noted what peace she seemed to have,
How tenderly she put flowers on his grave

But not as if he might return again
Or shine or seem quite close:
Rather to please us were the flowers she gave.

CHRISTOPHER MIDDLETON *b.* 1926

The Ancestors

When they come, we begin to go;
it's the ancestors,
they walk into the warm rooms,

eye our women and food, hear out
the good words. Then for words
and rooms we no more exist,

once the ancestors have come,
than a little dust on a vase,
than the breath wasted.

How do they come? They make no
parade of moans and winds;
they borrow no fears, none.

I am persuaded they have come
by the strength of shoes,
by the one shirt extra,

but if most by the bloody love
my shoes and my shirt need
to be seen that way,

I tell myself this is a thing
they'd far better not know,
who have lost the knack,

and only accuse, by the malice
they march us out with, from one
to the next lost place.

The Thousand Things

Dry vine leaves burn in an angle of the wall.
Dry vine leaves and a sheet of paper, overhung
by the green vine.
From an open grate in an angle of the wall
dry vine leaves and dead flies send smoke up
into the green vine where grape clusters go
ignored by lizards. Dry vine leaves
and a few dead flies on fire
and a Spanish toffee spat
into an angle of the wall
make a smell that calls to mind
the thousand things. Dead flies go,
paper curls and flares,
Spanish toffee sizzles and the smell
has soon gone over the wall.

A naked child jumps over the threshold,
waving a green spray of leaves of vine.

RICHARD MURPHY *b.* 1927

Girl at the Seaside

I lean on a lighthouse rock
Where the seagowns flow,
A trawler slips from the dock
Sailing years ago.

Wine, tobacco and seamen
Cloud the green air,
A head of snakes in the rain
Talks away desire.

A sailor kisses me
Tasting of mackerel,
I analyse misery
Till mass bells peal.

I wait for clogs on the cobbles,
Dead feet at night,
Only a tempest blows
Darkness on sealight.

I've argued myself here
To the blue cliff-tops:
I'll drop through the sea-air
Till everything stops.

FROM *The Battle of Aughrim*

"THE STORY I HAVE TO TELL"

The story I have to tell
Was told me by a teacher
Who read it in a poem
Written in a language that has died.
Two hundred and fifty years ago
The poet recalled
Meeting a soldier who had heard
From veterans of the war
The story I have to tell.

Deep red bogs divided
Aughrim, the horses' ridge
Of garland hedgerows and the summer dance,
Ireland's defence
From the colonists' advance.
Each saw his enemy across
A broad morass
Of godly bigotry and pride of race,
With a causeway two abreast could cross.

In opposite camps our ancestors
Ten marriages ago,
Caught in a feud of absent kings
Who used war like a basset table
Gambling to settle verbal things,
Decide if bread be God
Or God a parable,

Lit matchlocks, foddered horses, thirsted, marched,
Halted, and marched to battle.

"A COUNTRY WOMAN AND A COUNTRY MAN"

A country woman and a country man
Come to a well with pitchers,
The well that has given them water since they were children;
And there they meet soldiers.

Suspecting they've come to poison the spring
The soldiers decide to deal
Justly:
So they hang them on a tree by the well.

RAPPAREES

Out of the earth, out of the air, out of the water
And slinking nearer the fire, in groups they gather:
Once he looked like a bird, but now a beggar.

This fish-face leers from the trees: "Give me bread!"
He fins along the lake-shore with the starved.
Green eyes glow in the night from clumps of weed.

The water is still. A rock or the nose of an otter
Jars the surface. Whistle of rushes or bird?
It steers to the bank, it lands as a pikeman armed.

With flint and bundles of straw a limestone hall
Is gutted, a noble family charred in its sleep,
And they gloat by moonlight on a mound of rubble.

The highway trees are gibbets where seventeen rot
Who were caught last week in a cattle-raid.
The beasts are lowing. "Listen!" "Stifle the guard!"

In a pinewood thickness an earthed-over charcoal fire
Forges them guns. They melt lead stripped from a steeple
For ball. At the whirr of a snipe each can disappear

Terrified as a bird in a gorse-bush fire,
To delve like a mole or mingle like a nightjar
Into the earth, into the air, into the water.

CHARLES TOMLINSON *b.* 1927

Icos

White, a shingled path
Climbs among dusted olives
To where at the hill-crest
Stare houses, whiter
Than either dust or shingle.
The view, held from this vantage
Unsoftened by distance, because
Scoured by a full light,
Draws lucid across its depth
The willing eye: a beach,
A surf-line, broken
Where reefs meet it, into the heaving
Blanched rims of bay-arcs;
Above, piercing the empty blue,
A gull would convey whiteness
Through the sole space which lacks it
But, there, scanning the shore,
Hangs only the eagle, depth
Measured within its level gaze.

Four Kantian Lyrics

for Paul Roubiczek

1. *On a Theme of Pasternak*

I stared, but not to seize
the point of things: it was an incidental
sharpness held me there,
watching a sea of leaves
put out the sun. Spark
by spark, they drew it slowly down

sifting the hoard in glints
and pinheads. Rents of space
threatened to let it through
but, no—at once, the same
necessity that tamed the sky
to a single burning tone
would drag it deeper. Light
was suddenly beneath the mass
and silhouette of skirts and fringes,
shrinking to a glow on grass.
With dark, a breeze comes in
sends staggering the branches'
blackened ledges till they rear
recoiling. And now the trees are there
no longer, one can hear it climb
repeatedly their sullen hill
of leaves, rake and rouse them,
then their gathered tide
set floating all the house on air.

2. *What it was like*

It was like the approach of flame
treading the tinder, a fleet
cascade of it taking tree-toll,
halting below the hill and then
covering the corn-field's dryness
in an effortless crescendo. One heard
in the pause of the receding silence
the whole house grow
tense through its ties, the beams
brace beneath pantiles
for the coming burst. It came
and went. The blinded pane
emerged from the rainsheet
to an after-water world,
its green confusion brought
closer greener. The baptism
of the shining house was done
and it was like the calm

a church aisle harbours
tasting of incense, space and stone.

3. *An Insufficiency of Earth*

The wind goes over it. You see
the broken leaf-cope breathe
subsidingly, and lift itself
like water levelling. Stemmed,
this cloud of green, this mammoth
full of detail shifts
its shimmering, archaic head
no more. You think it for a second
hugely dead, until the ripple
soundless on the further corn,
is roaring in it. We cannot pitch
our paradise in such a changeful
nameless place and our encounters
with it. An insufficiency of earth
denies our constancy. For,
content with the iridescence of the moment,
we must flow with the wood-fleece
in a war of forms, the wind
gone over us, and we
drinking its imprints, faceless as the sea.

4. *How it happened*

It happened like this: I heard
from the farm beyond, a grounded
churn go down. The sound
chimed for the wedding of the mind
with what one could not see,
the further fields, the seamless
spread of space, and then,
all bestial ease, the cows
foregathered by the milking place
in a placid stupor. There are two
ways to marry with a land—
first, this bland and blind
submergence of the self, an act

of kind and questionless. The other
is the thing I mean, a whole
event, a happening, the sound
that brings all space in
for its bound, when self is clear
as what we keenest see and hear:
no absolute of eye can tell
the utmost, but the glance
goes shafted from us like a well.

The Fox

When I saw the fox, it was kneeling
in snow: there was nothing to confess
that, tipped on its broken forepaws
the thing was dead—save for its stillness.

A drift, confronting me, leaned down
across the hill-top field. The wind
had scarped it into a pennine wholly of snow, and
where did the hill go now?

There was no way round:
I drew booted legs
back out of it, took to my tracks again,
but already a million blown snow-motes were
     flowing and filling them in.

Domed at the summit, then tapering,
the drift still mocked
my mind as if the whole
fox-infested hill were the skull of a fox.

Scallops and dips
of pure pile rippled and shone, but what
should I do with such beauty
eyed by that?

It was like clambering between its white temples
as the crosswind tore
at one's knees, and each
missed step was a plunge at the hill's blinding interior.

THOMAS KINSELLA *b.* 1928

A *Country Walk*

Sick of the piercing company of women
I swung the gate shut with a furious sigh,
Rammed trembling hands in pockets and drew in
A breath of river air. A rook's wet wing
Cuffed abruptly upward through the drizzle.

On either hand dead trunks in drapes of creeper,
Strangled softly by horse-mushroom, writhed
In vanished passion, broken down like sponge.
I walked their hushed stations, passion dying,
Each slow footfall a drop of peace returning.

I clapped my gloves. Three cattle turned aside
Their fragrant bodies from a corner gate
And down the sucking chaos of a hedge
Churned land to liquid in their dreamy passage.
Briefly through the beaded grass a path
Led to the holy stillness of a well
And there in the smell of water, stone and leaf
I knelt, baring my hand, and scooped and drank,
Shivering, and inch by inch rejoiced:
Ferocity became intensity.

Or so it seemed as with a lighter step
I turned an ivied corner to confront
The littered fields where summer broke and fled.
Below me, right and left, the valley floor
Tilted in a silence full of storms;
A ruined aqueduct in delicate rigor
Clenched cat-backed, rooted to one horizon;
A vast asylum reared its potent calm
Up from the other through the sodden air,
Tall towers ochre where the gutters dripped;
A steeple; the long yielding of a railway turn
Through thorn and willow; a town endured its place . . .

Joining the two slopes, blocking an ancient way
With crumbled barracks, castle and brewery
It took the running river, wrinkling and pouring
Into its blunt embrace. A line of roofs
Fused in veils of rain and steely light
As the dying sun struck it huge glancing blows.
A strand of idle smoke mounted until
An idler current combed it slowly west,
A hook of shadow dividing the still sky . . .
Mated, like a fall of rock, with time,
The place endured its burden: as a froth
Locked in a swirl of turbulence, a shape
That forms and fructifies and dies, a wisp
That hugs the bridge, an omphalos of scraps.

I moved, my glove-backs glistening, over flesh-
And forest-fed earth; till, skirting a marshy field
Where melancholy brambles scored the mud
By the gapped glitter of a speckled ford,
I shuddered with a visual sweet excitement.

Those murmuring shallows made a trampling place
Apt for death-combat, as the tales agree:
There, the day that Christ hung dying, twin
Brothers armed in hate on either side;
The day darkened but they moved to meet
With crossed swords under a dread eclipse
And mingled their bowels at the saga's end.
There the first Normans massacred my fathers,
Then stroked their armoured horses' necks, disposed
In ceremony, sable on green sward.
Twice more the reeds grew red, the stones obscured;
When knot-necked Cromwell and his fervent sword
Despatched a convent shrieking to their Lover,
And when in peasant fear a rebel host,
Through long retreat grown half hysterical
—Methodical, ludicrous—piked in groups of three
Cromwell's puritan brood, their harmless neighbours,
Forked them half living to the sharp water
And melted into the martyred countryside,
Root eaters, strange as badgers. Pulses calmed;

The racked heroic nerved itself for peace;
Then came harsh winters, motionless waterbirds,
And generations that let welcome fail.

Road and river parted. Now my path
Lay gleaming through the greasy dusk, uphill
Into the final turn. A concrete cross
Low in the ditch grew to the memory
Of one who answered latest the phantom hag,
Tireless Rebellion, when with mouth awry
She hammered at the door, disrupting harvest.
There he bled to death, his line of sight
Blocked by the corner-stone, and did not see
His town ablaze with joy, the grinning foe
Driven in heavy lorries from the field;
And he lay cold in the Hill Cemetery
When freedom burned his comrades' itchy palms,
Too much for flesh and blood, and—armed in hate—
Brother met brother in a modern light.
They turned the bloody corner, knelt and killed,
Who gather still at Easter round his grave,
Our watchful elders. Deep in his crumbled heart
He takes their soil, and chatting they return
To take their town again, that have exchanged
A trenchcoat playground for a gombeen jungle.

Around the corner, in an open square,
I came upon the sombre monuments
That bear their names: MacDonagh & McBride,
Merchants; Connolly's Commercial Arms . . .
Their windows gave me back my stolid self
In attitudes of staring as I paced
Their otherworldly gloom, reflected light
Playing on lens and raincoat stonily.
I turned away. Down the sloping square
A lamp switched on above the urinal;
Across the silent handball alley, eyes
That never looked on lover measured mine
Over the Christian Brothers' frosted glass
And turned away. Out of the neighboring shades
A car plunged soundlessly and disappeared

Pitching downward steeply to the bridge.
I too descended. Naked sycamores,
Gathered dripping near the quay, stood still
And dropped from their combining arms a single
Word upon my upturned face. I trod
The river underfoot; the parapet
Above the central arch received my hands.

Under a darkening and clearing heaven
The hastening river streamed in a slate sheen,
Its face a-swarm. Across the swollen water
(Delicate myriads vanishing in a breath)
Faint ripples winked; a thousand currents broke,
Kissing, dismembering, in threads of foam
Or poured intact over the stony bed
Glass-green and chill; their shallow, shifting world
Slid on in troubled union, forging together
Surfaces that gave and swallowed light;
And grimly the flood divided where it swept
An endless debris through the failing dusk
Under the thudding span beneath my feet.
Venit Hesperus;
In green and golden light; bringing sweet trade.
The inert stirred. Heart and tongue were loosed:
"The waters hurtle through the flooded night . . ."

First Light

A prone couple still sleeps.
Light ascends like a pale gas
Out of the sea: dawn-
Light, reaching across the hill
To the dark garden. The grass
Emerges, soaking with grey dew.

Inside, in silence, an empty
Kitchen takes form, tidied and swept,
Blank with marriage—where shrill
Lover and beloved have kept
Another vigil far
Into the night, and raved and wept.

Upstairs a whimper or sigh
Comes from an open bedroom door
And lengthens to an ugly wail
—A child enduring a dream
That grows, at the first touch of day,
Unendurable.

Ritual of Departure

A man at the moment of departure, turning
To leave, treasures some stick of furniture
With slowly blazing eyes, or the very door
Broodingly with his hand as it falls shut.

*

Open the soft string that clasps in series
A dozen silver spoons, and spread them out,
Matched perfectly, one maker and to the year:
                              brilliance in use that fell
Open before the first inheritor.

A stag crest stares from the soft solid silver
And grimaces, with fat cud-lips but jaws
That could crack bones.
                              The stag heart stumbles.
He rears at bay, slavering silver; rattles
A trophied head among the gothic rocks.

*

Stones of a century and a half ago.
This same city distinct in the same air,
More open in an earlier evening light.
Dublin under the Georges . . .
                              stripped of Parliament,
Lying powerless in sweet-breathing death-ease
                              after forced Union.
Under a theatre of swift-moving cloud
Domes, pillared, in the afterglow—
A portico, beggars moving on the steps—
A horserider locked in soundless greeting,

Bowed among dogs and dung; the panelled vista
Closing on pleasant smoke-blue far-off hills.

*

The ground opens. Pale wet potatoes
Break into light. The black soil falls from their flesh,
From the hands that tear them up and spread them out
In fresh disorder, perishable roots to eat.
                              The fields vanish in rain
Among white rock and red bog—saturated
High places traversed by spring sleet
Or thrust up in summer through the thin wind
Into pounding silence. Farther south: cattle,
Wheat, salmon glistening, the sea.

Landscape with ancestral figures . . . names
Settling and intermixing on the earth,
The seed in slow retreat, through time and blood,
Into bestial silence.
                    Faces sharpen and grow blank,
With eyes for nothing.
                        And their children's children
Venturing to disperse, some came to Dublin
To vanish in the city lanes.
                            I saw the light
Enter from the laneway, through the scullery
To the foot of the stairs, creep across grey floorboards,
Sink in plush in the staleness of an inner room.

I scoop at the earth, and sense famine, a first
Sourness in the clay. The roots tear softly.

A. ALVAREZ *b.* 1929

Operation

"I'm bleeding. A boy, they said."
The town froze, close as a fist.
Winter was setting about us.

Like birds the bare trees shivered,
Birds without leaves or nests
As the fog took over.

My words were all gone, my tongue sour.
We sat in the car like the dead
Awaiting the dead. Your hair
Wept round your face like a willow
Unstirring. Your eyes were dry.

Unbodied, like smoke in the crowd,
You vanished. Later came violence,
Not that you felt it or cared,
Swaddled in drugs, apart
In some fractured, offensive dream,
While a bog-Irish nurse mopped up.

"Leave me. I'm bleeding. I bleed
Still. But he didn't hurt me."
Pale as the dead. As the dead
Fragile. Vague as the city
Now the fog chokes down again.
A life was pitched out like garbage.

"I bleed still. A boy, they said."
My blood stings like a river
Lurching over the falls.
My hands are bloody. My mind
Is rinsed with it. Blood fails me.
You lie like the dead, still bleeding,
While his fingers, unformed, unerring,
Hold us and pick us to pieces.

THOM GUNN b. 1929

On the Move

> "Man, you gotta Go."

The blue jay scuffling in the bushes follows
Some hidden purpose, and the gust of birds

That spurts across the field, the wheeling swallows,
Have nested in the trees and undergrowth.
Seeking their instinct, or their poise, or both,
One moves with an uncertain violence
Under the dust thrown by a baffled sense
Or the dull thunder of approximate words.

On motorcycles, up the road, they come:
Small, black, as flies hanging in heat, the Boys,
Until the distance throws them forth, their hum
Bulges to thunder held by calf and thigh.
In goggles, donned impersonality,
In gleaming jackets trophied with the dust,
They strap in doubt—by hiding it, robust—
And almost hear a meaning in their noise.

Exact conclusion of their hardiness
Has no shape yet, but from known whereabouts
They ride, direction where the tires press.
They scare a flight of birds across the field:
Much that is natural, to the will must yield.
Men manufacture both machine and soul,
And use what they imperfectly control
To dare a future from the taken routes.

It is a part solution, after all.
One is not necessarily discord
On earth; or damned because, half animal,
One lacks direct instinct, because one wakes
Afloat on movement that divides and breaks.
One joins the movement in a valueless world,
Choosing it, till, both hurler and the hurled,
One moves as well, always toward, toward.

A minute holds them, who have come to go:
The self-defined, astride the created will
They burst away; the towns they travel through
Are home for neither bird nor holiness,
For birds and saints complete their purposes.
At worst, one is in motion; and at best,
Reaching no absolute, in which to rest,
One is always nearer by not keeping still.

In Santa Maria del Popolo

Waiting for when the sun an hour or less
Conveniently oblique makes visible
The painting on one wall of this recess
By Caravaggio, of the Roman School,
I see how shadow in the painting brims
With a real shadow, drowning all shapes out
But a dim horse's haunch and various limbs,
Until the very subject is in doubt.

But evening gives the act, beneath the horse
And one indifferent groom, I see him sprawl,
Foreshortened from the head, with hidden face,
Where he has fallen, Saul becoming Paul.
O wily painter, limiting the scene
From a cacophony of dusty forms
To the one convulsion, what is it you mean
In that wide gesture of the lifting arms?

No Ananias croons a mystery yet,
Casting the pain out under name of sin.
The painter saw what was, an alternate
Candor and secrecy inside the skin.
He painted, elsewhere, that firm insolent
Young whore in Venus' clothes, those pudgy cheats,
Those sharpers; and was strangled, as things went,
For money, by one such picked off the streets.

I turn, hardly enlightened, from the chapel
To the dim interior of the church instead,
In which there kneel already several people,
Mostly old women: each head closeted
In tiny fists holds comfort as it can.
Their poor arms are too tired for more than this
—For the large gesture of solitary man,
Resisting, by embracing, nothingness.

JOHN MONTAGUE *b.* 1929

The First Invasion of Ireland

for Michael Walsh

According to Leabhar Gabhàla, *the Book of Conquests, the first invasion of Ireland was by relatives of Noah, just before the Flood. Refused entry into the Ark, they consulted an idol which told them to flee to Ireland. There were three men and fifty-one women in the party and their behaviour has so little common with subsequent tradition in Ireland that one must take the story to be mythological.*

Fleeing from threatened flood, they sailed,
Seeking the fair island, without serpent or claw;
From the deck of their hasty windjammer watched
The soft edge of Ireland nearward draw.

A sweet confluence of waters, a trinity of rivers,
Was their first resting place:
They unloaded the women and the sensual idol,
Guiding image of their disgrace.

Division of damsels they did there,
The slender, the tender, the dimpled, the round,
It was the first just bargain in Ireland,
There was enough to go round.

Lightly they lay and pleasured
In the green grass of that guileless place:
Ladhra was the first to die;
He perished of an embrace.

Bith was buried in a stone heap,
Riot of mind, all passion spent.
Fintan fled from the ferocious women
Before he, too, by love was rent.

Great primitive princes of our line
They were the first, with stately freedom,
To sleep with women in Ireland:
Soft the eternal bed they lie upon.

On a lonely headland the women assembled,
Chill as worshippers in a nave,
And watched the eastern waters gather
Into a great virile flooding wave.

All Legendary Obstacles

All legendary obstacles lay between
Us, the long imaginary plain,
The monstrous ruck of mountains
And, swinging across the night,
Flooding the Sacramento, San Joaquin,
The hissing drift of winter rain.

All day I waited, shifting
Nervously from station to bar
As I saw another train sail
By, the San Francisco Chief or
Golden Gate, water dripping
From great flanged wheels.

At midnight you came, pale
Above the negro porter's lamp.
I was too blind with rain
And doubt to speak, but
Reached from the platform
Until our chilled hands met.

You had been travelling for days
With an old lady, who marked
A neat circle on the glass
With her glove, to watch us
Move into the wet darkness
Kissing, still unable to speak.

The Trout

for Barrie Cooke

Flat on the bank I parted
Rushes to ease my hands
In the water without a ripple
And tilt them slowly downstream
To where he lay, light as a leaf,
In his fluid sensual dream.

Bodiless lord of creation
I hung briefly above him
Savouring my own absence
Senses expanding in the slow
Motion, the photographic calm
That comes before action.

As the curve of my hands
Swung under his body
He surged, with visible pleasure.
I was so preternaturally close
I could count every stipple
But still cast no shadow, until

The two palms crossed in a cage.
Under the lightly pulsing gills.
Then (entering my own enlarged
Shape, which rode on the water)
I gripped. To this day I can
Taste his terror on my hands.

TED HUGHES *b.* 1930

November

The month of the drowned dog. After long rain the land
Was sodden as the bed of an ancient lake,

Treed with iron and birdless. In the sunk lane
The ditch—a seep silent all summer—

Made brown foam with a big voice: that, and my boots
On the lane's scrubbed stones, in the gulleyed leaves,
Against the hill's hanging silence;
Mist silvering the droplets on the bare thorns

Slower than the change of daylight.
In a let of the ditch a tramp was bundled asleep:
Face tucked down into beard, drawn in
Under its hair like a hedgehog's. I took him for dead,

But his stillness separated from the death
Of the rotting grass and the ground. A wind chilled,
And a fresh comfort tightened through him,
Each hand stuffed deeper into the other sleeve.

His ankles, bound with sacking and hairy band,
Rubbed each other, resettling. The wind hardened;
A puff shook a glittering from the thorns,
And again the rains' dragging grey columns

Smudged the farms. In a moment
The fields were jumping and smoking; the thorns
Quivered, riddled with the glassy verticals.
I stayed on under the welding cold

Watching the tramp's face glisten and the drops on his coat
Flash and darken. I thought what strong trust
Slept in him—as the trickling furrows slept,
And the thorn-roots in their grip on darkness;

And the buried stones, taking the weight of winter;
The hill where the hare crouched with clenched teeth.
Rain plastered the land till it was shining
Like hammered lead, and I ran, and in the rushing wood

Shuttered by a black oak leaned.
The keeper's gibbet had owls and hawks
By the neck, weasels, a gang of cats, crows:
Some, stiff, weightless, twirled like dry bark bits

In the drilling rain. Some still had their shape,
Had their pride with it; hung, chins on chests,
Patient to outwait these worst days that beat
Their crowns bare and dripped from their feet.

Pike

Pike, three inches long, perfect
Pike in all parts, green tigering the gold.
Killers from the egg: the malevolent aged grin.
They dance on the surface among the flies.

Or move, stunned by their own grandeur,
Over a bed of emerald, silhouette
Of submarine delicacy and horror.
A hundred feet long in their world.

In ponds, under the heat-struck lily pads—
Gloom of their stillness:
Logged on last year's black leaves, watching upwards.
Or hung in an amber cavern of weeds

The jaws' hooked clamp and fangs
Not to be changed at this date;
A life subdued to its instrument;
The gills kneading quietly, and the pectorals.

Three we kept behind glass,
Jungled in weed: three inches, four,
And four and a half: fed fry to them—
Suddenly there were two. Finally one

With a sag belly and the grin it was born with.
And indeed they spare nobody.
Two, six pounds each, over two feet long,
High and dry and dead in the willow-herb—

One jammed past its gills down the other's gullet:
The outside eye stared: as a vise locks—
The same iron in this eye
Though its film shrank in death.

A pond I fished, fifty yards across,
Whose lilies and muscular tench
Had outlasted every visible stone
Of the monastery that planted them—

Stilled legendary depth:
It was as deep as England. It held
Pike too immense to stir, so immense and old
That past nightfall I dared not cast

But silently cast and fished
With the hair frozen on my head
For what might move, for what eye might move.
The still splashes on the dark pond,

Owls hushing the floating woods
Frail on my ear against the dream
Darkness beneath night's darkness had freed,
That rose slowly towards me, watching.

An Otter

I

Underwater eyes, an eel's
Oil of water body, neither fish nor beast is the otter:
Four-legged yet water-gifted, to outfish fish;
With webbed feet and long ruddering tail
And a round head like an old tomcat.

Brings the legend of himself
From before wars or burials, in spite of hounds and vermin-poles;
Does not take root like the badger. Wanders, cries;
Gallops along land he no longer belongs to;
Re-enters the water by melting.

Of neither water nor land. Seeking
Some world lost when first he dived, that he cannot come at since,
Takes his changed body into the holes of lakes;
As if blind, cleaves the stream's push till he licks
The pebbles of the source; from sea

To sea crosses in three nights
Like a king in hiding. Crying to the old shape of the starlit land,
Over sunken farms where the bats go round,
Without answer. Till light and birdsong come
Walloping up roads with the milk wagon.

II

The hunt's lost him. Pads on mud,
Among sedges, nostrils a surface bead,
The otter remains, hours. The air,
Circling the globe, tainted and necessary,

Mingling tobacco-smoke, hounds and parsley,
Comes carefully to the sunk lungs.
So the self under the eye lies,
Attendant and withdrawn. The otter belongs

In double robbery and concealment—
From water that nourishes and drowns, and from land
That gave him his length and the mouth of the hound.
He keeps fat in the limpid integument

Reflections live on. The heart beats thick,
Big trout muscle out of the dead cold;
Blood is the belly of logic; he will lick
The fishbone bare. And can take stolen hold

On a bitch otter in a field full
Of nervous horses, but linger nowhere.
Yanked above hounds, reverts to nothing at all,
To this long pelt over the back of a chair.

Cadenza

The violinist's shadow vanishes.

The husk of a grasshopper
Sucks a remote cyclone and rises.

The full, bared throat of a woman walking water,
The loaded estuary of the dead.

And I am the cargo
Of a coffin attended by swallows.

And I am the water
Bearing the coffin that will not be silent.

The clouds are full of surgery and collisions
But the coffin escapes—as a black diamond,

A ruby brimming blood,
An emerald beating its shores,

The sea lifts swallow wings and flings
A summer lake open,

Sips and bewilders its reflection,
Till the whole sky dives shut like a burned land back to its spark—

A bat with a ghost in its mouth
Struck at by lightnings of silence—

Blue with sweat, the violinist
Crashes into the orchestra, which explodes.

JON SILKIN *b.* 1930

Someone I Lost

(For a sadistic girl)

One night you did not arrive;
And though the phone, like a dead man, tingled the air
You never answered once.
But then I found you lying exhausted in the
Sleep of the hunted.
You had been with those prim, sadistic creatures.

Old men and their half-wived daughters
On whom no rod is sacred but for pain.
So smear your grit about

The belly and hope it sticks in the cut flesh; no shame
　　Appeases the ancient cupidon
Whose tongue and whose trunk, its sticks fallow and pallid

　　By fifty years,
Would split the tender flesh as you would with cane open the cheeks
　　Of another's flesh.
Assuage you his whips then; there is no scorn like a child's
　　Scorn no, nor cruelty
The child will invent to perform though impotent to

　　The globe of love's tear.
Today is yesterday and today's gift is more pain;
　　So inflict what you care
To lash into corporeal, childish hate
　　That temporal hate for yourself.
For I do not care that that whip which you turn through your flesh

　　As the moon her shade through your brain,
Swells her flesh, like a deformity into some rose,
　　Rose, as you would say, beautiful
If red. Yet I know there is never a face but all other
　　Memory, like a fish
In the dark slips my straining hands; see, your face is a lamp

　　Shut from this fisherman's gaze
　　Though his lamp swings close.

GEORGE MacBETH *b*. 1932

The Return

　　　After the light has set
　First I imagine silence: then the stroke
　As if some drum beat outside has come in.
　And in the silence I smell moving smoke
　And feel the touch of coarse cloth on my skin.
　　　And all is darkness yet
　Save where the hot wax withers by my chin.

When I had fallen (bone
Bloodying wet stone) he would lead me back
Along the street and up the corkscrew stair
(Time running anti-clockwise, fingers slack)
And open windows to let in fresh air
   And leave me stretched alone
With sunken cheeks drained whiter than my hair.

   Then I was young. Before
Another stroke he will come back in bone
And thin my heart. That soot-black hill will break
And raise him in his clay suit from the stone
While my chalk-ridden fingers dryly ache
   And burn. On this rush floor
He will come striding hotly. When I wake

   The stroke will have been tolled
And I shall take his crushed purse in my hand
And feel it pulse (warm, empty) on my wrist.
Blood floods my temples. Clay man, from what land
Have you come back to keep your freezing tryst
   With someone grown so old?
Soldier, forgive me. Candles die in mist.

   And now a cold wind stirs
Inside the shuttered room. I feel his hand
Brushing the stale air, feeling for my place
Across the phlegm-soaked pillows. I am sand
Threading a glass with slow and even pace
   And dying in my furs.
My father turns, with tears on his young face.

Scissor-Man

   I am dangerous
     in a crisis
   with sharp legs and a screw

     in my genitals. I slice
   bacon-rind for a living. At nights I
   lie dried

under the draining-board, dreaming
          of Nutcrackers
and the Carrot-grater. If I should

          catch him rubbing
those tin nipples of hers
          in the bread-bin

(God rust his pivot!) so much for
          secrecy. I'd have his
washer off. And

          then what? It scarcely pays
to be "Made In Hamburg." Even
          our little salt-spoon

can sound snooty
          with an E.P.N.S. under
his armpit. Even the pie-server

          who needs re-dipping. In sixteen
stainless years dividing
          chippolata-links I

am still denied
          a place in the sink unit. And
you can imagine

          what pairing-off is possible
with a wriggle of cork-screws
          in an open knife-box. So I

keep my legs
          crossed. I never cut up
rough. I lie with care

          in a world where a squint leg
could be fatal. I sleep like a weapon
          with a yen for a pierced ear.

PETER REDGROVE *b.* 1932

Against Death

We are glad to have birds in our roof
Sealed off from rooms by white ceiling,
And glad to glimpse them homing straight
Blinking across the upstairs windows,
And to listen to them scratching on the laths
As we bed and whisper staring at the ceiling.
We're glad to be hospitable to birds.
In our rooms, in general only humans come,
We keep no cats and dislike wet-mouthed dogs,
And wind comes up the floorboards in a gale,
So then we keep to bed: no more productive place
To spend a blustery winter evening and keep warm.
Occasionally a spider capsises in the bath,
Blot streaming with legs among the soap,
Cool and scab-bodied, soot-and-suet,
So we have to suffocate it down the pipe
For none of us'd have dealings with it,
Like kissing a corpse's lips, even
Through the fingers, so I flood it out.
In our high-headed rooms we're going to breed
Many human beings for their home
To fill the house with children and with life,
Running in service of the shrill white bodies,
With human life but for sparrows in the roof,
Wiping noses and cleaning up behind,
Slapping and sympathising, and catching glimpses
Of each other and ourselves as we were then,
And let out in the world a homing of adults.
And if there ever should be a corpse in the house
Hard on its bedsprings in a room upstairs,
Smelling of brass-polish, with sucked-in cheeks,
Staring through eyelids at a scratching ceiling,
Some firm'd hurry it outdoors and burn it quick—
We'd expect no more to happen to ourselves

Our children gradually foregoing grief of us
As the hot bodies of the sparrows increase each summer.

Dismissal

She dismisses me in late sunbeams
In the meadow mealy with life.
Pollens, smoking, mingle,
All the thin flowers shuffle,
Stagger with rummaging throngs.
I am attentive to my sentence,
Attention is my mask;
I march to the fringe of the wood.

My feeling is worn out.
She fidgets like a husk
Blown askance in a web of hair,
Pale, frowning and white-necked.
My step just clips a bee
Which sizzles, and plucks free.

Thick roots strap the soil.
I trash mushrooms at each step
That were not there last night
White-headed and wry-necked.
A husk on a gossamer
Snaps across my sight,
Gibbets on my wink,
And I catch through gasps in the leaves
As the sun couches on breeze
All the small clouds like thin masks
Shucking lightly into dark.

The American
Poets

RAMON GUTHRIE *b.* 1896

The Clown: He Dances in the Clearing by Night

He took his wig off, with his sleeve
wiped painted snigger from his face
and did a dance you'd not believe . . .
with easy-jointed limpid pace
wove through such figures as the eye
could scarcely follow, whistling slow
a tune of scant variety
like whispers on a piccolo.

The Tyger in his forest stared,
chin sunk upon his powered paws
while pirouette and caper dared
the awesome sinews of the Laws
his stripèd humors improvise—
Immutabilities laid down
by conclaves of eternities—
revoked an instant by the Clown.

He danced the twittering of quails
and dolphins' pleasure in the sea
and planets screaming on their rails
of finely drawn infinity.
Then naked, having cast aside
motley of Time and Space and Number,
he glided silent through the wide
vistas of the Tyger's slumber.

Laura Age Eight: She falls asleep across the arm of a sofa.

When this young *objet trouvé* improvises sleep
she formulates new definitions
     of grace and even comfort

as absurd
                    and vice versa
as they are authentic

          Eyelashes against contour of a
cheek and nose tip
                    coiled limber spine
sprawled disrupted skein of
                    elbows   knees   shins
                                        sneakered feet
mane whose pendant weight
               would be wasted on a pillow

This abrupt repose is of no single kingdom
                    Cats and catkins have it
          colts and ferns and wild
columbine

          And in the mineral realm
some of the more improbably
               spontaneous
                              crystals

          Patterns akin to this sometimes turn up
on beaches
               as intricately twined
roots of driftwood.

KENNETH REXROTH *b.* 1905

Doubled Mirrors

          It is the dark of the moon.
          Late at night, the end of summer,
          The autumn constellations
          Glow in the arid heaven.
          The air smells of cattle, hay,
          And dust. In the old orchard

The pears are ripe. The trees
Have spouted from old rootstocks
And the fruit is inedible.
As I pass them I hear something
Rustling and grunting and turn
My light into the branches.
Two raccoons with acrid pear
Juice and saliva drooling
From their mouths stare back at me,
Their eyes deep sponges of light.
They know me and do not run
Away. Coming up the road
Through the black oak shadows, I
See ahead of me, glinting
Everywhere from the dusty
Gravel, tiny points of cold
Blue light, like the sparkle of
Iron snow. I suspect what it is,
And kneel to see. Under each
Pebble and oak leaf is a
Spider, her eyes shining at
Me with my reflected light
Across immeasurable distance.

THEODORE ROETHKE 1908–1963

Orchids

They lean over the path
Adder-mouthed,
Swaying close to the face,
Coming out, soft and deceptive,
Limp and damp, delicate as a young bird's tongue;
Their fluttery fledgling lips
Move slowly,
Drawing in the warm air.

And at night,
The faint moon falling through whitewashed glass,
The heat going down
So their musky smell comes even stronger,
Drifting down from their mossy cradles:
So many devouring infants!
Soft luminescent fingers,
Lips neither dead nor alive,
Loose ghostly mouths
Breathing.

Give Way, Ye Gates

1

Believe me, knot of gristle, I bleed like a tree;
I dream of nothing but boards;
I could love a duck.

Such music in a skin!
A bird sings in the bush of your bones.
Tufty, the water's loose.
Bring me a finger. This dirt's lonesome for grass.
Are the rats dancing? The cats are.
And you, cat after great milk and vasty fishes,
A moon loosened from a stag's eye,
Twiced me nicely,—
In the green of my sleep,
In the green.

2

Mother of blue and the many changes of hay,
This tail hates a flat path.
I've let my nose out;
I could melt down a stone,—
How is it with the long birds?
May I look too, loved eye?
It's a wink beyond the world.

In the slow rain, who's afraid?
We're king and queen of the right ground.
I'll risk the winter for you.

You tree beginning to know,
You whisper of kidneys,
We'll swinge the instant!—
With jots and jogs and cinders on the floor:
The sea will be there, the great squashy shadows,
Biting themselves perhaps;
The shrillest frogs;
And the ghost of some great howl
Dead in a wall.
In the high-noon of thighs,
In the springtime of stones,
We'll stretch with the great stems.
We'll be at the business of what might be
Looking toward what we are.

3

You child with a beast's heart,
Make me a bird or a bear!
I've played with the fishes
Among the unwrinkling ferns
In the wake of a ship of wind;
But now the instant ages,
And my thought hunts another body.
I'm sad with the little owls.

4

Touch and arouse. Suck and sob. Curse and mourn.
It's a cold scrape in a low place.
The dead crow dries on a pole.
Shapes in the shade
Watch.

The mouth asks. The hand takes.
These wings are from the wrong nest.
Who stands in a hole
Never spills.

I hear the clap of an old wind.
The cold knows when to come.
What beats in me
I still bear.

The deep stream remembers:
Once I was a pond.
What slides away
Provides.

CHARLES OLSON *b.* 1910

The Kingfishers

1

What does not change / is the will to change

He woke, fully clothed, in his bed. He
remembered only one thing, the birds, how
when he came in, he had gone around the rooms
and got them back in their cage, the green one first,
she with the bad leg, and then the blue,
the one they had hoped was a male

Otherwise? Yes, Fernand, who had talked lispingly of
        Albers & Angkor Vat.
He had left the party without a word. How he got up, got into his coat,
I do not know. When I saw him, he was at the door, but it did not
        matter,
he was already sliding along the wall of the night, losing himself
in some crack of the ruins. That it should have been he who said,
        "The kingfishers!
who cares
for their feathers
now?"

His last words had been, "The pool is slime." Suddenly everyone,
ceasing their talk, sat in a row around him, watched

they did not so much hear, or pay attention, they
wondered, looked at each other, smirked, but listened,
he repeated and repeated, could not go beyond his thought
"The pool   the kingfishers' feathers were wealth   why
did the export stop?"

It was then he left

2

I thought of the E on the stone, and of what Mao said
la lumière"
        but the kingfisher
de l'aurore"
        but the kingfisher flew west
est devant nous!
        he got the color of his breast
        from the heat of the setting sun!

The features are, the feebleness of the feet (syndactylism of the 3rd &
    4th digit)
the bill, serrated, sometimes a pronounced beak, the wings
where the color is, short and round, the tail
inconspicuous.

But not these things were the factors. Not the birds.
The legends are
legends. Dead, hung up indoors, the kingfisher
will not indicate a favoring wind,
or avert the thunderbolt. Nor, by its nesting,
still the waters, with the new year, for seven days.
It is true, it does nest with the opening year, but not on the waters.
It nests at the end of a tunnel bored by itself in a bank. There,
six or eight white and translucent eggs are laid, on fishbones
not on bare clay, on bones thrown up in pellets by the birds.

                On these rejectamenta
(as they accumulate they form a cup-shaped structure) the young
    are born.
And, as they are fed and grow, this nest of excrement and decayed
    fish becomes
                a dripping, fetid mass

Mao concluded:
>   nous devons
>   nous lever
>   et agir!

3

When the attentions change / the jungle
leaps in
>   even the stones are split
>   they rive

Or,
enter
that other conqueror we more naturally recognize
he so resembles ourselves

But the E
cut so rudely on that oldest stone
sounded otherwise,
was differently heard

as, in another time, were treasures used:

(and, later, much later, a fine ear thought
a scarlet coat)

>   "of green feathers   feet, beaks and eyes
>   of gold

>   "animals likewise,
>   resembling snails

>   "a large wheel, gold, with figures of unknown four-foots,
>   and worked with tufts of leaves, weight
>   3800 ounces

>   "last, two birds, of thread and featherwork, the quills
>   gold, the feet
>   gold, the two birds perched on two reeds
>   gold, the reeds arising from two embroidered mounds,

one yellow, the other
white.

"And from each reed hung
seven feathered tassels.

In this instance, the priests
(in dark cotton robes, and dirty,
their dishevelled hair matted with blood, and flowing wildly
over their shoulders)
rush in among the people, calling on them
to protect their gods

And all now is war
where so lately there was peace,
and the sweet brotherhood, the use
of tilled fields.

4

Not one death but many,
not accumulation but change, the feed-back proves, the feed-back is
the law

Into the same river no man steps twice
When fire dies air dies
No one remains, nor is, one

Around an appearance, one common model, we grow up
many. Else how is it,
if we remain the same,
we take pleasure now
in what we did not take pleasure before? love
contrary objects? admire and/or find fault? use
other words, feel other passions, have
nor figure, appearance, disposition, tissue
the same?

To be in different states without a change
is not a possibility

We can be precise. The factors are
in the animal and/or the machine the factors are

communication and/or control, both involve
the message. And what is the message? The message is
a discrete or continuous sequence of measurable events distributed in
    time

is the birth of air, is
the birth of water, is
a state between
the origin and
the end, between
birth and the beginning of
another fetid nest

is change, presents
no more than itself

And the too strong grasping of it,
when it is pressed together and condensed,
loses it

This very thing you are

II

    They buried their dead in a sitting posture
    serpent   cane   razor   ray of the sun

    And she sprinkled water on the head of the child, crying
    "Cioa-coatl! Cioa-coatl!"
    with her face to the west

    Where the bones are found, in each personal heap
    with what each enjoyed, there is always
    the Mongolian louse

The light is in the east. Yes. And we must rise, act. Yet
in the west, despite the apparent darkness (the whiteness
which covers all), if you look, if you can bear, if you can, long enough

        as long as it was necessary for him, my guide
        to look into the yellow of that longest-lasting rose

so you must, and, in that whiteness, into that face, with what candor,
    look

and, considering the dryness of the place
    the long absence of an adequate race

        (of the two who first came, each a conquistador, one healed,
            the other
        tore the eastern idols down, toppled
        the temple walls, which, says the excuser
        were black from human gore)

hear
hear, where the dry blood talks
    where the old appetite walks

                la più saporita e migliore
                che si possa trovar al mondo

where it hides, look
in the eye how it runs
in the flesh / chalk

        but under these petals
        in the emptiness
        regard the light, contemplate
        the flower

whence it arose

        with what violence benevolence is bought
        what cost in gesture justice brings
        what wrongs domestic rights involve
        what stalks
        this silence

        what pudor pejorocracy affronts
        how awe, night-rest and neighborhood can rot
        what breeds where dirtiness is law
        what crawls
        below

III

    I am no Greek, hath not th'advantage.
    And of course, no Roman:

he can take no risk that matters,
the risk of beauty least of all.

But I have my kin, if for no other reason than
(as he said, next of kin) I commit myself, and,
given my freedom, I'd be a cad
if I didn't. Which is most true.

It works out this way, despite the disadvantage.
I offer, in explanation, a quote:
si j'ai du goût, ce n'est guère
que pour la terre et les pierres

Despite the discrepancy (an ocean   courage   age)
this is also true: if I have any taste
it is only because I have interested myself
in what was slain in the sun

    I pose you your question:

shall you uncover honey / where maggots are?

    I hunt among stones

Maximus, to Himself

I have had to learn the simplest things
last. Which made for difficulties.
Even at sea I was slow, to get the hand out, or to cross
a wet deck.
        The sea was not, finally, my trade.
But even my trade, at it, I stood estranged
from that which was most familiar. Was delayed,
and not content with the man's argument
that such postponement
is now the nature of
obedience,
        that we are all late
        in a slow time,
        that we grow up many
        And the single

is not easily
known

It could be, though the sharpness (the *achiote*)
I note in others,
makes more sense
than my own distances. The agilities

they show daily
who do the world's
businesses
And who do nature's
as I have no sense
I have done either

I have made dialogues,
have discussed ancient texts,
have thrown what light I could, offered
what pleasures
doceat allows

But the known?
This, I have had to be given,
a life, love, and from one man
the world.

Tokens.
But sitting here
I look out as a wind
and water man, testing
And missing
some proof

I know the quarters
of the weather, where it comes from,
where it goes. But the stem of me,
this I took from their welcome,
or their rejection, of me

And my arrogance
was neither diminished
nor increased,
by the communication

2

It is undone business
I speak of, this morning,
with the sea
stretching out
from my feet

The Moebius Strip

Upon a Moebius strip
materials and the weights of pain
their harmony

A man within himself upon an empty ground.
His head lay heavy on a huge right hand
itself a leopard on
his left and angled shoulder.
His back a stave, his side a hole into the bosom of a sphere.

His head passed down a sky (as suns the circle of a year).
His other shoulder, open side and thigh maintained,
by law of conservation of
the graveness of his center,
their clockwise fall.
Then he knew, so came to apogee
and earned and wore himself as amulet.

I saw another man lift up a woman in his arms
he helmeted, she naked too, protected as Lucrece by her alarms.
Her weight tore down his right and muscled thigh
but they in turn returned upon the left
to carry violence outcome in her eye.
It was his shoulder that sustained, the right,
bunched as by buttocks or by breasts,
and gave them back the leisure of their rape.

And three or four who danced,
so joined as triple-thighed and bowed and arrowed folk
who spilled their pleasure once as yoke
on stone-henge plain.

Their bare and lovely bodies sweep, in round
of viscera, of legs
of turned-out hips and glance, bound
each to other, nested eggs
of elements in trance.

ELIZABETH BISHOP *b.* 1911

Arrival at Santos

Here is a coast; here is a harbor;
here, after a meager diet of horizon, is some scenery:
impractically shaped and—who knows?—self-pitying mountains,
sad and harsh beneath their frivolous greenery,

with a little church on top of one. And warehouses,
some of them painted a feeble pink, or blue,
and some tall, uncertain palms. Oh, tourist,
is this how this country is going to answer you

and your immodest demands for a different world,
and a better life, and complete comprehension
of both at last, and immediately,
after eighteen days of suspension?

Finish your breakfast. The tender is coming,
a strange and ancient craft, flying a strange and brilliant rag.
So that's the flag. I never saw it before.
I somehow never thought of there *being* a flag,

but of course there was, all along. And coins, I presume,
and paper money; they remain to be seen.
And gingerly now we climb down the ladder backward,
myself and a fellow passenger named Miss Breen,

descending into the midst of twenty-six freighters
waiting to be loaded with green coffee beans.
Please, boy, do be more careful with that boat hook!
Watch out! Oh! It has caught Miss Breen's

skirt! There! Miss Breen is about seventy,
a retired police lieutenant, and six feet tall,
with beautiful bright blue eyes and a kind expression.
Her home, when she is at home, is in Glens Fall

s, New York. There. We are settled.
The customs officials will speak English, we hope,
and leave us our bourbon and cigarettes.
Ports are necessities, like postage stamps, or soap,

but they seldom seem to care what impression they make,
or, like this, only attempt, since it does not matter,
the unassertive colors of soap, or postage stamps—
wasting away like the former, slipping the way the latter

do when we mail the letters we wrote on the boat,
either because the glue here is very inferior
or because of the heat. We leave Santos at once;
we are driving to the interior.

PAUL GOODMAN *b.* 1911

Poems of My Lambretta

1

This pennant new
   my motorbike will fly:
a sea of icy blue
   and a pale blue sky
      and in the sky the wan
      yellow midnight sun,

Sally stitched for me
   of sturdy cloth
and silk embroidery
   to flaunt when forth
      I roar, so me all men
      may know by my emblem.

2

My new license plate
is thirty zip six
orange and black
and cost me two bucks.

Castor and Pollux,
from cops preserve me
and all encounters
involving insurance.

Through lovely landscape
guide my wheels
and may my buddy-seat
carry friendly freight.

3

Dirty and faded
  is the banner of my bike
and tattered in the winds
  of journey like

my self-esteem my soiled
  repute my faded hope.
The little motor but
  briskly roars me up

the hills and not half-way
  like some on Helicon.
Yet I recall a day
  she balked and stood there dumb.

It was no use to kick
  and swear at her. At her
own moment lightly she
  coughs, and off we roar!

on glad our windy way
  nowhere, going forty!
Flapping is my flag,
  faded torn and dirty,

and on the buddy-seat
    there rides Catullus dead
and speaks to me in gusts of shouts,
    I dare not turn my head.

4

Oh we had the April evenings!
I had to tear myself away
a hasty kiss and on my way
past past the Cadillacs
that passed the Fords that passed the trucks,
I never had to jam the brakes
for I am a New Yorker bred,
the light is green all my road.
High in the forehead of the South
before me blazed in the lilac dust
the Evening Star and I was drunk
on speed and the memory of your musk.
That was before I had the flat
and now the goddam clutch sticks
and you have gone to Bloomington.

BROTHER ANTONINUS *b.* 1912

In All These Acts

*Cleave the wood and thou shalt find Me, lift the rock and I am
there!*   The Gospel According to Thomas

Dawn cried out: the brutal voice of a bird
Flattened the seaglaze. Treading that surf
Hunch-headed fishers toed small agates,
Their delicate legs, iridescent, stilting the ripples.
Suddenly the cloud closed. They heard big wind
Boom back on the cliff, crunch timber over along the ridge.
They shook up their wings, crying; terror flustered their pinions.
Then hemlock, tall, torn by the roots, went crazily down,
The staggering gyrations of splintered kindling.

Flung out of bracken, fleet mule deer bolted;
But the great elk, caught midway between two scissoring logs,
Arched belly-up and died, the snapped spine
Half torn out of his peeled back, his hind legs
Jerking that gasped convulsion, the kick of spasmed life,
Paunch plowed open, purple entrails
Disgorged from the basketwork ribs
Erupting out, splashed sideways, wrapping him,
Gouted in blood, flecked with the brittle sliver of bone.
Frenzied, the terrible head
Thrashed off its antlered fuzz in that rubble
And then fell still, the great tongue
That had bugled in rut, calling the cow-elk up from the glades,
Thrust agonized out, the maimed member
Bloodily stiff in the stone-smashed teeth . . .

                              Far down below,
The mountain torrent, that once having started
Could never be stopped, scooped up that avalanchial wrack
And strung it along, a riddle of bubble and littered duff
Spun down its thread. At the gorged river mouth
The sea plunged violently in, gasping its potholes,
Sucked and panted, answering itself in its spume.
The river, spent at last, beating driftwood up and down
In a frenzy of capitulation, pumped out its life,
Destroying itself in the mother sea,
There where the mammoth sea-grown salmon
Lurk immemorial, roe in their hulls, about to begin.
They will beat that barbarous beauty out
On those high-stacked shallows, those headwater claims,
Back where they were born. Along that upward-racing trek
Time springs through all its loops and flanges,
The many-faced splendor and the music of the leaf,
The copulation of beasts and the watery laughter of drakes,
Too few the grave witnesses, the wakeful, vengeful beauty,
Devolving itself of its whole constraint,
Erupting as it goes.

                    In all these acts
Christ crouches and seethes, pitched forward
On the crucifying stroke, juvescent, that will spring Him

Out of the germ, out of the belly of the dying buck,
Out of the father-phallus and the torn-up root.
These are the modes of His forth-showing,
His serene agonization. In the clicking teeth of otters
Over and over He dies and is born,
Shaping the weasel's jaw in His leap
And the staggering rush of the bass.

MURIEL RUKEYSER *b.* 1913

Waterlily Fire

for Richard Griffith

I. *The Burning*

Girl grown woman   fire   mother of fire
I go the stone street turning to fire.   Voices
Go screaming   Fire   to the green glass wall.
And there where my youth flies blazing into fire
The   dance   of sane and insane images, noon
Of seasons and days.   Noontime of my one hour.

Saw down the bright noon street the crooked faces
Among the tall daylight in the city of change.
The scene has walls   stone   glass   all my gone life
One wall a web through which the moment walks
And I am open, and the opened hour
The world as water-garden   lying behind it.
In a city of stone, necessity of fountains,
Forced water fallen on glass, men with their axes.

An arm of flame reaches from water-green glass,
Behind the wall I know waterlilies
Drinking their light, transforming light and our eyes
Skythrown under water, clouds under those flowers,
Walls standing on all things stand in a city noon
Who will not believe a waterlily fire.

Whatever can happen in a city of stone,
Whatever can come to a wall can come to this wall.

I walk in the river of crisis toward the real,
I pass guards, finding the center of my fear
And you, Dick, endlessly my friend during storm.

The arm of flame striking through the wall of form.

II. *The Island*

Born of this river and this rock island, I relate
The changes   :   I born when the whirling snow
Rained past the general's grave and the amiable child
White past the windows of the house of Gyp the Blood.
General, gangster, child.   I know in myself the island.

I was the island without bridges, the child down whose blazing
Eye the men of plumes and bone raced their canoes and fire
Among the building of my young childhood, houses;
I was those changes, the live darknesses
Of wood, the pale grain of a grove in the fields
Over the river fronting red cliffs across—
And always surrounding her the river, birdcries, the wild
Father building his sand, the mother in panic her parks—
Bridges were thrown across, the girl arose
From sleeping streams of change in the change city.
The violent forgetting, the naked sides of darkness.
Fountain of a city in growth, an island of light and water.
Snow striking up past the graves, the yellow cry of spring.

Whatever can come to a city can come to this city.

Under the tall compulsion
                    of the past
I see the city
            change like a man changing
I love this man
            with my lifelong body of love
I know you
            among your changes
                        wherever I go

Hearing the sounds of building
                              the syllables of wrecking
A young girl watching
                         the man throwing red hot rivets
Coals in a bucket of change
How can you love a city that will not stay?
I love you
              like a man of life in change.

Leaves like yesterday shed, the yellow of green spring
Like today accepted and become one's self
I go, I am a city with bridges and tunnels,
Rock, cloud, ships, voices. To the man where the river met
The tracks, now buried deep along the Drive
Where blossoms like sex pink, dense pink, rose, pink, red.

Towers falling.   A dream of towers.
Necessity of fountains.   And my poor,
Stirring among our dreams,
Poor of my own spirit, and tribes, hope of towers
And lives, looking out through my eyes.
The city the growing body of our hate and love,
The root of the soul, and war in its black doorways.
A male sustained cry interrupting nightmare.
Male flower heading upstream.

Among a city of light, the stone that grows.
Stigma of dead stone, inert water, the tattered
Monuments rivetted against flesh.
Blue noon where the wall made big agonized men
Stand like sailors pinned howling on their lines, and I
See stopped in time a crime behind green glass,
Lilies of all my life on fire.
Flash faith in a city building its fantasies.

I walk past the guards into my city of change.

III. *Journey Changes*

Many of us   Each in his own life waiting
Waiting to move   Beginning to move   Walking
And early on the road of the hill of the world

Come to my landscapes emerging on the grass

The stages of the theatre of the journey

I see the time of willingness between plays
Waiting and walking and the play of the body
Silver body with its bosses and places
One by one touched awakened into into

Touched and turned one by one into   flame

The theatre of the advancing goddess   Blossoming
Smiles as she stands intensely being in stillness
Slowness in her blue dress advancing standing I go
And far across a field over the jewel grass

The play of the family stroke by stroke acted out

Gestures of deep acknowledging on the journey stages
Of the playings the play of the goddess and the god
A supple god of searching and reaching
Who weaves his strength   Who dances her more alive

The theatre of all animals, my snakes, my great horses

Always the journey   long   patient   many haltings
Many waitings for choice and again easy breathing
When the decision to go on is made
Along the long slopes of choice and again the world

The play of poetry approaching in its solving

Solvings of relations in poems and silences
For we were born to express   born for a journey
Caves, theatres, the companioned solitary way
And then I came to the place of mournful labor

A turn in the road and the long sight from the cliff

Over the scene of the land dug away to nothing and many
Seen to a stripped horizon carrying barrows of earth
A hod of earth taken and emptied and thrown away
Repeated farther than sight.   The voice saying slowly

But it is hell.   I heard my own voice in the words
Or it could be a foundation   And after the words
My chance came.   To enter.   The theatres of the world.

IV. *Fragile*

I think of the image brought into my room
Of the sage and the thin young man who flickers and asks.
He is asking about the moment when the Buddha
Offers the lotus, a flower held out as declaration.
"Isn't that fragile?" he asks.   The sage answers:
"I speak to you.   You speak to me.   Is that fragile?"

V. *The Long Body*

This journey is exploring us. Where the child stood
An island in a river of crisis, now
The bridges bind us in symbol, the sea
Is a bond, the sky reaches into our bodies.
We pray : we dive into each other's eyes.

Whatever can come to a woman can come to me.

This is the long body : into life from the beginning,
Big-headed infant unfolding into child, who stretches and finds
And then flowing the young one going tall, sunward,
And now full-grown, held, tense, setting feet to the ground,
Going as we go in the changes of the body,
As it is changes, in the long strip of our many
Shapes, as we range shifting through time.
The long body : a procession of images.

This moment in a city, in its dream of war.
                    We chose to be,
Becoming the only ones under the trees
                    when the harsh sound
Of the machine sirens spoke. There were these two men,
And the bearded one, the boys, the Negro mother feeding
Her baby. And threats, the ambulances with open doors.
Now silence. Everyone else within the walls. We sang.
            We are the living island,
We the flesh of this island, being lived,
Whoever knows us is part of us today.

Whatever can happen to anyone can happen to me.

Fire striking its word among us, waterlilies
Reaching from darkness upward to a sun
Of rebirth, the implacable.   And in our myth
The Changing Woman who is still and who offers.

Eyes drinking light, transforming light, this day
That struggles with itself, brings itself to birth.
In ways of being, through silence, sources of light
Arriving behind my eye, a dialogue of light.

And everything a witness of the buried life.
This moment flowing across the sun, this force
Of flowers and voices body in body through space.
The city of endless cycles of the sun.

I speak to you   You speak to me

DELMORE SCHWARTZ 1913–1966

All of the Fruits Had Fallen

All of the fruits had fallen,
The bears had fallen asleep,
And the pears were useless and soft
Like used hopes, under the starlight's
Small knowledge, scattered aloft
In a glittering senseless drift:
The jackals of remorse in a cage
Drugged beyond mirth and rage.

Then, then, the dark hour flowered!
Under the silence, immense
And empty as far-off seas,
I wished for the innocence
Of my stars and my stones and my trees
All the brutality and inner sense

A dog and a bird possess,
The dog who barked at the moon
As an enemy's white fang,
The bird that thrashed up the bush
And soared to soar as it sang,
A being all present as touch,
Free of the future and past
—Until, in the dim window glass,
The fog or cloud of my face
Showed me my fear at last!

JOHN BERRYMAN *b.* 1914

Dream Song 29

There sat down, once, a thing on Henry's heart
só heavy, if he had a hundred years
& more, & weeping, sleepless, in all them time
Henry could not make good.
Starts again always in Henry's ears
the little cough somewhere, an odour, a chime.

And there is another thing he has in mind
like a grave Sienese face a thousand years
would fail to blur the still profiled reproach of. Ghastly,
with open eyes, he attends, blind.
All the bells say: too late. This is not for tears;
thinking.

But never did Henry, as he thought he did,
end anyone and hacks her body up
and hide the pieces, where they may be found.
He knows: he went over everyone, & nobody's missing.
Often he reckons, in the dawn, them up.
Nobody is ever missing.

Dream Song 53

He lay in the middle of the world, and twitcht.
More Sparine for Pelides,
human (half) & down here as he is,
with probably insulting mail to open
and certainly unworthy words to hear
and his unforgivable memory.

—I seldom *go* to *films*. They are too exciting,
said the Honourable Possum.
—It takes me so long to read the 'paper,
said to me one day a novelist hot as a firecracker,
because I have to identify myself with everyone in it,
including the corpses, pal.

Kierkegaard wanted a society, to refuse to read 'papers,
and that was not, friends, his worst idea.
Tiny Hardy, toward the end, refused to say *anything*,
a programme adopted early on by long Housman,
and Gottfried Benn
said: —We are using our own skins for wallpaper and we cannot win.

RANDALL JARRELL 1914–1965

Windows

Quarried from snow, the dark walks lead to doors
That are dark and closed. The white- and high-roofed houses
Float in the moonlight of the shining sky
As if they slept, the bedclothes pulled around them.
But in some the lights still burn. The lights of others' houses.

Those who live there move seldom, and are silent.
Their movements are the movements of a woman darning,
A man nodding into the pages of the paper,

And are portions of a rite—have kept a meaning—
That I, that they know nothing of. What I have never heard
He will read me; what I have never seen
She will show me.
                As dead actors, on a rainy afternoon,
Move in a darkened living-room, for children
Watching the world that was before they were,
The windowed ones within their windowy world
Move past me without doubt and for no reason.

These actors, surely have known nothing of today,
That time of troubles and of me. Of troubles.
Morose and speechless, voluble with elation,
Changing, unsleeping, an unchanging speech,
These have not lived; look up, indifferent,
At me at my window, from the snowy walk
They move along in peace. . . . If only I were they!
Could act out, in longing, the impossibility
That haunts me like happiness!

Of so many windows, one is always open.

Some morning they will come downstairs and find me.
They will start to speak, and then smile speechlessly,
Shifting the plates, and set another place
At a table shining by a silent fire.
When I have eaten they will say, "You have not slept."

And from the sofa, mounded in my quilt,
My face on *their* pillow, that is always cool,
I will look up speechlessly into a—

It blurs, and there is drawn across my face
As my eyes close, a hand's slow fire-warmed flesh.

It moves so slowly that it does not move.

WILLIAM STAFFORD *b.* 1914

Elegy

The responsible sound of the lawnmower
puts a net under the afternoon;
closing the refrigerator door
I hear a voice in the other room
that starts up color in every cell:
    Presents like this, Father, I got from you,
    and there are hundreds more to tell.

One night, sound held in cornfield farms
drowned in August, and melonflower breath
creeping in stealth—we walked west
where all the rest of the country slept.
I hold that memory in both my arms—
    how the families there had starved the dogs;
    in the night they waited to be fed.

At the edge of dark there paled a flash—
a train came on with its soft tread
that roused itself with light and thundered
with dragged windows curving down earth's side
while the cornstalks whispered.
    All of us hungry creatures watched
    until it was extinguished.

If only once in all those years
the right goodby could have been said!
I hear you climbing up the snow,
a brown-clad wanderer on the road
with the usual crooked stick,
    and on the wrong side of the mountains
    I can hear the latches click.

Remember in the Southwest going down the canyons?
We turned off the engine, the tires went hoarse
picking up sound out of turned away mountains;

we felt the secret sky lean down.
Suddenly the car came to with a roar.
>   And remember the Christmas wreath on our door—
>   when we threw it away and it jumped blue up the fire?

At sight of angels or anything unusual
you are to mark the spot with a cross,
for I have set out to follow you
and these marked places are expected,
but in between I can hear no sound.
>   The softest hush of doors I close
>   may jump to slam in a March wind.

When you left our house that night and went falling
into that ocean, a message came: silence.
I pictured you going, spangles and bubbles
leaving your pockets in a wheel clockwise.
Sometimes I look out of our door at night.
>   When you send messages they come spinning
>   back into sound with just leaves rustling.

Come battering. I listen, am the same, waiting.

THEODORE WEISS *b.* 1916

Ruins for These Times

I

To hell with holy relics,
sniffing like some mangy dog
after old, dead scents (saints?),
those that went this way before
and went. More shambling about
in abandoned, clammy churches
and I abjure all religion,
even my own!
>   It's much too late

to heft a Yorick skull and, ear
to it as to a surf-mad-shell,
hold forth foul breath to breath
on man's estate.
                    What's more
I, plundered, plundering,
out of these forty odd bumbling
years have heaped up spoils
with spells compelling
enough, my own:
                    a father
who keeps coming apart however
I try to patch him together
again. Old age too much for him,
the slowly being picked to pieces
as a boy with a fly, he hopped
a spunky horse and left
change gaping in the dust.
                    Mother
too who would not watch herself
turn into blind and stinking
stone, took things into her own
hands, finished a rotten job
with a rush.

                    II

                    But lest I seem
too personal, let me cite
the grand, efficient, ruin-making
fashion of our time.
                    This earth,
a star, brave and portly once,
now like a chimney belches
filthiest smoke, fallout
of roasting human meat the air
we breathe;
                    the ember-eyes
of millions I have never seen
(yet relatives the more for this,
stand-ins for the role

I missed by sheerest accident)
flare up within my dream's
effective dark.
                    O let Odysseus,
Hamlet, and their sparkling
ilk grope after; here's
a midnight ought to satisfy
the genius in them.

III

                    Let them.
What's the mess of Europe,
late or antique, great or antic,
to the likes of me?
                    Pottering
about in my own cluttered memory,
I turn up, still in full career,
my grandfather, muscles sprung
from dragging packs through miles
of factories:
                    a grandmother
who bore, conscripted lifelong
to the total war of hunger
and a strange new world,
three families on her back
and then outwore them all
as she outwore her ailments,
one enough to fell a warrior:

that friend whose breath shaped
songs desperately debonair
out of our snarling dog-eat-dog
accomplishments.

IV

                    There too
I poke out bits, still standing,
from my wrecks, begun in fervor,
aspiration, joy:
                    those passages

through which the morning strode,
enlightened in its retinue,
choke on the plaster falling,
raspy stenches, refuse of lives
trapped in them.
                Is the building
lust for ruin so strong in those gone
before that I and mine are nothing
but a story added, foundation
for new ruins?
               The prospect
that seemed the way to heaven
glimmers mainly with the promise
of a final storm, a monument
of glittering bones to gratify
most dogged fates.
                   Our own.

ROBERT LOWELL *b.* 1917

To Delmore Schwartz

Cambridge 1946

We couldn't even keep the furnace lit!
Even when we had disconnected it,
the antiquated
refrigerator gurgled mustard gas
through your mustard-yellow house,
and spoiled our long maneuvered visit
from T. S. Eliot's brother, Henry Ware. . . .

Your stuffed duck craned toward Harvard from my trunk:
its bill was a black whistle, and its brow
was high and thinner than a baby's thumb;
its webs were tough as toenails on its bough.
It was your first kill; you had rushed it home,

pickled in a tin wastebasket of rum—
it looked through us, as if it'd died dead drunk.
You must have propped its eyelids with a nail,
and yet it lived with us and met our stare,
Rabelaisian, lubricious, drugged. And there,
perched on my trunk and typing-table,
it cooled our universal
Angst a moment, Delmore. We drank and eyed
the chicken-hearted shadows of the world.
Underseas fellows, nobly mad,
we talked away our friends. "Let Joyce and Freud,
the Masters of Joy,
be our guests here," you said. The room was filled
with cigarette smoke circling the paranoid,
inert gaze of Coleridge, back
from Malta—his eyes lost in flesh, lips baked and black.
Your tiger kitten, *Oranges*,
cartwheeled for joy in a ball of snarls.
You said:
"*We poets in our youth begin in sadness;
thereof in the end come despondency and madness;*
Stalin has had two cerebral hemorrhages!"
The Charles
River was turning silver. In the ebb-
light of morning, we stuck
the duck
-'s web-
foot, like a candle, in a quart of gin we'd killed.

Man and Wife

Tamed by *Miltown*, we lie on Mother's bed;
the rising sun in war paint dyes us red;
in broad daylight her gilded bed-posts shine,
abandoned, almost Dionysian.
At last the trees are green on Marlborough Street,
blossoms on our magnolia ignite
the morning with their murderous five days' white.
All night I've held your hand,
as if you had

a fourth time faced the kingdom of the mad—
its hackneyed speech, its homicidal eye—
and dragged me home alive. . . . Oh my *Petite*,
clearest of all God's creatures, still all air and nerve:
you were in your twenties, and I,
once hand on glass,
and heart in mouth,
outdrank the Rahvs in the heat
of Greenwich Village, fainting at your feet—
too boiled and shy
and poker-faced to make a pass,
while the shrill verve
of your invective scorched the traditional South.

Now twelve years later, you turn your back.
Sleepless, you hold
your pillow to your hollows like a child;
your old-fashioned tirade—
loving, rapid, merciless—
breaks like the Atlantic Ocean on my head.

Water

It was a Maine lobster town—
each morning boatloads of hands
pushed off for granite
quarries on the islands,

and left dozens of bleak
white frame houses stuck
like oyster shells
on a hill of rock,

and below us, the sea lapped
the raw little match-stick
mazes of a weir,
where the fish for bait were trapped.

Remember? We sat on a slab of rock.
From this distance in time,

it seems the color
of iris, rotting and turning purpler,

but it was only
the usual gray rock
turning the usual green
when drenched by the sea.

The sea drenched the rock
at our feet all day,
and kept tearing away
flake after flake.

One night you dreamed
you were a mermaid clinging to a wharf-pile,
and trying to pull
off the barnacles with your hands.

We wished our two souls
might return like gulls
to the rock. In the end,
the water was too cold for us.

Fall 1961

Back and forth, back and forth
goes the tock, tock, tock
of the orange, bland, ambassadorial
face of the moon
on the grandfather clock.

All autumn, the chafe and jar
of nuclear war;
we have talked our extinction to death.
I swim like a minnow
behind my studio window.

Our end drifts nearer,
the moon lifts,
radiant with terror.
The state
is a diver under a glass bell.

A father's no shield
for his child.
We are like a lot of wild
spiders crying together,
but without tears.

Nature holds up a mirror.
One swallow makes a summer.
It's easy to tick
off the minutes,
but the clockhands stick.

Back and forth!
Back and forth, back and forth—
my one point of rest
is the orange and black
oriole's swinging nest!

ROBERT DUNCAN *b.* 1919

After a Passage in Baudelaire

Ship, leaving or arriving, of my lover,
my soul, leaving or coming into this harbor,
among your lights and shadows   shelterd,
at home in your bulk, the cunning
regularity and symmetry thruout
of love's design, of will, of your
attractive cells and chambers

riding forward, darkest of shades
over the shadowd waters
into the light, neat, symmetrically
arranged above your watery reflections
disturbing your own image, moving as you are

What passenger, what sailor,
looks out into the swirling currents round you
as if into those depths into a mirror?

What lights in what port-holes
raise in my mind again   hunger and impatience?
to make my bed down again, there, beyond me,
as if this room too, my bedroom, my lamp at my side,
were among those lights sailing out
                   away from me.

We too, among the others, passengers
in that *charme infini et mystérieux,*
in that suitable symmetry, that precision
everywhere, the shining fittings, the fit
of lights and polisht surfaces to the dark,
to the flickering shadows of them,
we too, unfaithful to me, sailing away,
leaving me.

L'idée poétique, the idea of a poetry,
that rises from the movement, from the
outswirling curves and imaginary figures
round this ship, this fate, this sure thing,

est l'hypothèse d'une être vaste, immense,

compliqué, mais eurythmique.

Strains of Sight

1

He brought a light so she could see
Adam move nakedly in the lighted room.
It was a window in the tree.
It was a shelter where there was none.

She saw his naked back and thigh
and heard the notes of a melody
where Adam out of his nature came
into four walls, roof and floor.

He turnd on the light and turnd back,
moving with grace to match her eye.
She saw his naked loneliness.

Now I shall never rest, she sighd,
until he strips his heart for me.
The body flashes such thoughts of death
so that time leaps up, and a man's hand

seen naked catches upon my breath
the risk we took in Paradise.
The serpent thought before the tomb
laid naked, naked, naked before the eyes,

reflects upon itself in a bare room.

2

In the questioning phrase the voice
—he raises his eyes from the page—
follows towards some last
curve of the air, suspended above

its sign, that point, that
And asks, Who am I then?
Where am I going? There is no time
like now that is not like now.

Who?   turns upon some body where
the hand striving to tune
curves of the first lute whose strings are nerves
sees in the touch the phrase will

rise . break
as the voice does? above some moving obscurity

ripples out in the disturbd pool,
shadows and showings where we would read
—raising his eyes from the body's lure—

what the question is,
where the heart reflects.

Shelley's Arethusa *Set to New Measures*

1

Now Arethusa from her snow couches arises,
Hi! from her Acroceraunian heights springs,
down leaping, from cloud and crag
jagged shepherds her bright fountains.
She bounds from rock-face to rock-face streaming
her uncombd rainbows of hair round her.
> Green paves her way-fare.
> Where she goes there
> dark ravine serves her
> downward towards the West-gleam.
As if still asleep she goes, glides or
> lingers in deep pools.

2

> Now bold Alpheus
> aroused from his cold glacier
strikes the mountains and opens
> a chasm in the rock so that
all Erymanthus shakes, and the black
> south wind is unseald,
from urns of silent snow comes. Earthquake
> rends asunder
thunderous the bars of the springs below.

Beard and hair of the River-god
> show through the torrent's sweep
where he follows the fleeting-light of the nymph
> to the brink of the Dorian,
> margins of deep Ocean.

3

> *Oh save me! Take me untoucht*, she cries.
> *Hide me*,
for *Alpheus already grasps at my hair!*
> The loud Ocean heard,
to its blue depth stirrd and divided,

taking her into the roar of its surf.
    And under the water she flees,
    white Arethusa,
the sunlight still virginal in her courses,
    Earth's daughter, descends,
billowing, unblended in the Dorian
    brackish waters.

       Where Alpheus,
    close upon her, in gloom,
    staining the salt dark tides comes,
black clouds overtaking the white
    in an emerald sky, Alpheus
eagle-eyed down streams of the wind pursues
    dove-wingd Arethusa.

4

    Under those bowers they go
    where the ocean powers
brood on their thrones. Thru these coral woods,
    shades in the weltering flood,
    maiden and raging
    Alpheus swirl.

Over forgotten heap, stone upon stone,
    thru dim beams
    which amid streams
weave a network of colord lights they go,
    girl-stream and man-river after her.

    Pearl amid shadows
    of the deep caves
that are green as the forest's night,
    swift they fly,
with the shark and the swordfish pass into the wave
    —he overtaking her,
    as if wedding, surrounding her,
spray rifts in clefts of the shore cliffs rising.

    Alpheus,
        Arethusa,
            come home.

5

When now from Enna's mountains they spring,
    afresh in her innocence
Arethusa to Alpheus gladly comes.
Into one morning two hearts awake,
    at sunrise leap from sleep's caves to return
        to the vale where they meet,
drawn by yearning from night into day.

Down into the noontide flow,
    into the full of life winding again, they find
their way thru the woods
    and the meadows of asphodel below.
Wedded, one deep current leading,
    they follow to dream
in the rocking deep at the Ortygian shore.

    Spirits drawn upward,
        they are divided
into the azure from which the rain falls,
    life from life,
seeking their way to love once more.

LAWRENCE FERLINGHETTI *b.* 1919

Away above a harborful

Away above a harborful
                        of caulkless houses
among the charley noble chimneypots
                        of a rooftop rigged with clotheslines
        a woman pastes up sails
                        upon the wind
    hanging out her morning sheets
                        with wooden pins
            O lovely mammal
                        her nearly naked teats

throw taut shadows
                    when she stretches up
to hang at last the last of her
                    so white washed sins
        but it is wetly amorous
                            and winds itself about her
            clinging to her skin
                            So caught with arms upraised
        she tosses back her head
                            in voiceless laughter
    and in choiceless gesture then
                            shakes out gold hair

while in the reachless seascape spaces

                        between the blown white shrouds

    stand out the bright steamers

                        to kingdom come

MAY SWENSON *b.* 1919

Seeing the Frog

Seeing the frog
and on its back
embroidery like eyes,
I felt it "see" me
also as shadow
in disguise.

Lengthening
without motion
carefully my hand
lowered a socket—
and unclosed a pond.

Memory handed me
a frog,
pulse under thumb:
how to hold
a loose thing tight,
yet not lame.

The jerk, the
narrow hips' escape
happened again.
I felt the chill
embossment and
the ticking chin.

Before the splash
a hand spread
in whole design,
tan and shadow-
patched, the warts
of water mine!

HOWARD NEMEROV *b.* 1920

The Mud Turtle

Out of the earth beneath the water,
Dragging over the stubble field
Up to the hilltop in the sun
On his way from water to water,
He rests an hour in the garden,
His alien presence observed by all:
His lordly darkness decked in filth
Bearded with weed like a lady's favor.
He is a black planet, another world
Never till now appearing, even now
Not quite believably old and big,
Set in the summer morning's midst

A gloomy gemstone to the sun opposed.
Our measures of him do not matter,
He would be huge at any size;
And neither does the number of his years,
The time he comes from doesn't count.

When the boys tease him with sticks
He breaks the sticks, striking with
As great a suddenness as speed;
Fingers and toes would snap as soon,
Says one of us, and the others shudder.
Then when they turn him on his back
To see the belly heroically yellow,
He throws himself fiercely to his feet,
Brings down the whole weight of his shell,
Spreads out his claws and digs himself in
Immovably, invulnerably,
But for the front foot on the left,
Red-budded, with the toes torn off.
So over he goes again, and shows
Us where a swollen slug is fastened
Softly between plastron and shell.
Nobody wants to go close enough
To burn it loose; he can't be helped
Either, there is no help for him
As he makes it to his feet again
And drags away to the meadow's edge.
We see the tall grass open and wave
Around him, it closes, he is gone
Over the hill toward another water
Bearing his hard and chambered hurt
Down, down, down, beneath the water,
Beneath the earth beneath. He takes
A secret wound out of the world.

JAMES SCHEVILL *b.* 1920

Death of a Cat

A sultry, summer evening, the children playing jacks
    in the hot and grimy garage
    under the yellow eyes of their grey cat,
    when the rubbery jack ball
    popped like a bubble into the street
And the cocky cat after its red-streaking path.

Brakes scrunched, the cat shot up like a spark,
    hit harshly over a tilted ear,
    and the cross-legged children screamed
    at the driven death of their pet.
    While I hauled a hose to clean
The clotted pavement stains, I thought of an ancient legend.

In the Irish Golden Age, three fasting clerks on pilgrimage
    sailed hungrily off to sea,
    praying with soft and folded hands
    their serene faith in God's care.
    But the young clerk said in his caution,
"I think I will take the silence of my small, grey cat."

On the rocky shore of an island, they beached the boat
    and kneeled to speak the Psalms;
    the cat crept to a wild wave
    and snatched a salmon from the foam.
    Still the clerks doubted the Lord's hand
Until the fish began to burn upon a sudden fire of coals.

Kneeling shadowy on the oily pavement, I saw
    some jelly of the cat's lost brain,
    a little mound of curious cells
    clinging against the asphalt veins
    and fountainhead of lashing water.
Only the hose's full fury washed the cells away.

The myth of the showering, supernal claw grew old
  in the grey silence of evening.
  lost in the glittering air;
  though as water smashed the cells,
  they flickered in tingling twilight
Like sparks snapping through the foam of a fire.

HAYDEN CARRUTH *b.* 1921

On a Certain Engagement South of Seoul

A long time, many years, we've had these wars.
When they were opened, one can scarcely say.
We were high school students, no more than sophomores,

When Italy broke her peace on a dark day,
And that was not the beginning. The following years
Grew crowded with destruction and dismay.

When I was nineteen, once the surprising tears
Stood in my eyes and stung me, for I saw
A soldier in a newsreel clutch his ears

To hold his face together. Those that paw
The public's bones to eat the public's heart
Said far too much, of course. The sight, so raw

And unbelievable, of people blown apart
Was enough to numb us without that bark and whine.
We grew disconsolate. Each had his chart

To mark on the kitchen wall the battle-line,
But many were out of date. The radio
Droned through the years, a faithful anodyne.

Yet the news of this slight encounter somewhere below
Seoul stirs my remembrance: we were a few,
Sprawled on the stiff grass of a small plateau,

Afraid. No one was dead. But we were new—
We did not know that probably none would die.
Slowly, then, all vision went askew.

My clothing was outlandish; earth and sky
Were metallic and horrible. We were unreal,
Strange bodies and alien minds; we could not cry

For even our eyes seemed to be made of steel;
Nor could we look at one another, for each
Was a sign of fear, and we could not conceal

Our hatred for our friends. There was no speech.
We sat alone, all of us, trying to wake
Some memory of the selves beyond our reach.

That place was conquered. The nations undertake
Another campaign now, in another land,
A stranger land perhaps. And we forsake

The miseries there that we can't understand
Just as we always have. And yet my glimpse
Of a scene on the distant field can make my hand

Tremble again. How quiet we are. One limps.
One cannot walk at all. Or one is all right.
But one owns this experience that crimps

Forgetfulness, especially at night.
Is this a bond? Does this make us brothers?
Or does it bring our hatred back? I might

Have known, but now I do not know. Others
May know. I know when I walk out-of-doors
I have a sorrow not wholly mine, but another's.

RICHARD WILBUR *b.* 1921

Advice to a Prophet

When you come, as you soon must, to the streets of our city,
Mad-eyed from stating the obvious,
Not proclaiming our fall but begging us
In God's name to have self-pity,

Spare us all word of the weapons, their force and range,
The long numbers that rocket the mind;
Our slow, unreckoning hearts will be left behind,
Unable to fear what is too strange.

Nor shall you scare us with talk of the death of the race.
How should we dream of this place without us?—
The sun mere fire, the leaves untroubled about us,
A stone look on the stone's face?

Speak of the world's own change. Though we cannot conceive
Of an undreamt thing, we know to our cost
How the dreamt cloud crumbles, the vines are blackened by
        frost,
How the view alters. We could believe,

If you told us so, that the white-tailed deer will slip
Into perfect shade, grown perfectly shy,
The lark avoid the reaches of our eye,
The jack-pine lose its knuckled grip

On the cold ledge, and every torrent burn
As Xanthus once, its gliding trout
Stunned in a twinkling. What should we be without
The dolphin's arc, the dove's return,

These things in which we have seen ourselves and spoken?
Ask us, prophet, how we shall call
Our natures forth when that live tongue is all
Dispelled, that glass obscured or broken

In which we have said the rose of our love and the clean
Horse of our courage, in which beheld
The singing locust of the soul unshelled,
And all we mean or wish to mean.

Ask us, ask us whether with the worldless rose
Our hearts shall fail us; come demanding
Whether there shall be lofty or long standing
When the bronze annals of the oak-tree close.

JAMES DICKEY *b.* 1923

The Firebombing

> *Denke daran, dass nach den grossen Zerstörungen*
> *Jedermann beweisen wird, dass er unschuldig war.*
> —*Günter Eich*
>
> *Or hast thou an arm like God?*
> —The Book of Job

Homeowners unite.

All families lie together, though some are burned alive.
The others try to feel
For them. Some can, it is often said.

Starve and take off

Twenty years in the suburbs, and the palm trees willingly leap
Into the flashlights,
And there is beneath them also
A booted crackling of snailshells and coral sticks.
There are cowl flaps and the tilt cross of propellers,
The shovel-marked clouds' far sides against the moon,
The enemy filling up the hills
With ceremonial graves. At my somewhere among these,

Snap, a bulb is tricked on in the cockpit

And some technical-minded stranger with my hands
Is sitting in a glass treasure-hole of blue light,
Having potential fire under the undeodorized arms
Of his wings, on thin bomb-shackles,
The "tear-drop-shaped" 300-gallon drop-tanks
Filled with napalm and gasoline.

Thinking forward ten minutes
From that, there is also the burst straight out
Of the overcast into the moon; there is now
The moon-metal-shine of propellers, the quarter-
moonstone, aimed at the waves,
Stopped on the cumulus.

There is then this re-entry
Into cloud, for the engines to ponder their sound.
In white dark the aircraft shrinks; Japan

Dilates around it like a thought.
Coming out, the one who is here is over
Land, passing over the all-night grainfields,
In dark paint over
The woods with one silver side,
Rice-water calm at all levels
Of the terraced hill.
                          Enemy rivers and trees
Sliding off me like snakeskin,
Strips of vapor spooled from the wingtips
Going   invisible   passing   over   on
Over   bridges   roads for nightwalkers
Sunday night in the enemy's country   absolute
Calm   the moon's face   coming   slowly
About
          the inland sea
Slants   is woven with wire thread
Levels out   holds together like a quilt
Off the starboard wing   cloud flickers
At my glassed-off forehead   the moon's now and again
Uninterrupted face going forward
Over the waves in a glide-path
Lost into land.

Going: going with it

Combat booze by my side in a cratered canteen,
Bourbon frighteningly mixed
With GI pineapple juice,
Dogs trembling under me for hundreds of miles, on many
Islands, sleep-smelling that ungodly mixture
Of napalm and high-octane fuel,
Good bourbon and GI juice.

Rivers circling behind me around
Come to the fore, and bring
A town with everyone darkened.
Five-thousand people are sleeping off
An all-day American drone.
Twenty years in the suburbs have not shown me
Which ones were hit and which not.

Haul on the wheel   racking slowly
The aircraft blackly around
In a dark dream   that   that is
That is like flying inside someone's head

Think of this   think of this

I did not think of my house
But think of my house now

Where the lawn mower rests on its laurels
Where the diet exists
For my own good   where I try to drop
Twenty years, eating figs in the pantry
Blinded by each and all
Of the eye-catching cans that gladly have caught my wife's eye
Until I cannot say
Where the screwdriver is   where the children
Get off the bus   where the new
Scoutmaster lives   where the fly
Hones his front legs   where the hammock folds
Its erotic daydreams   where the Sunday
School text for the day has been put   where the fire
Wood is   where the payments

For everything under the sun
Pile peacefully up,

But in this half-paid-for pantry
Among the red lids that screw off
With an easy half-twist to the left
And the long drawers crammed with dim spoons,
I still have charge—secret charge—
Of the fire developed to cling
To everything: to golf carts and fingernail
Scissors as yet unborn   tennis shoes
Grocery baskets   toy fire engines
New Buicks stalled by the half-moon
Shining at midnight on crossroads   green paint
Of jolly garden tools   red Christmas ribbons:

Not atoms, these, but glue inspired
By love of country to burn,
The apotheosis of gelatin.

Behind me having risen the Southern Cross
Set up by chaplains in the Ryukyus—
Orion, Scorpio, the immortal silver
Like myths of king-
insects at swarming time—
One mosquito, dead drunk
On altitude, drones on, far under the engines,
And bites between
The oxygen mask and the eye.
The enemy-colored skin of families
Determines to hold its color
In sleep, as my hand turns whiter
Than ever, clutching the toggle—
The ship shakes   bucks
Fire hangs   not yet fire
In the air above Beppu
For I am fulfilling

An "anti-morale" raid upon it.
All leashes of dogs
Break under the first bomb, around those
In bed, or late in the public baths: around those

Who inch forward on their hands
Into medicinal waters.
Their heads come up with a roar
Of Chicago fire:
Come up with the carp pond showing
The bathhouse upside down,
Standing stiller to show it more
As I sail artistically over
The resort town followed by farms,
Singing and twisting
All the handles in heaven   kicking
The small cattle off their feet
In a red costly blast
Flinging jelly over the walls
As in a chemical war-
fare field demonstration.
With fire of mine like a cat

Holding onto another man's walls,
My hat should crawl on my head
In streetcars, thinking of it,
The fat on my body should pale.

Gun down
The engines, the eight blades sighing
For the moment when the roofs will connect
Their flames, and make a town burning with all
American fire.
              Reflections of houses catch;
Fire shuttles from pond to pond
In every direction, till hundreds flash with one death.
With this in the dark of the mind,
Death will not be what it should;
Will not, even now, even when
My exhaled face in the mirror
Of bars, dilates in a cloud like Japan.
The death of children is ponds
Shutter-flashing; responding mirrors; it climbs
The terraces of hills
Smaller and smaller, a mote of red dust
At a hundred feet; at a hundred and one it goes out.

That is what should have got in
To my eye

And shown the insides of houses, the low tables
Catch fire from the floor mats,
Blaze up in a gas around their heads
Like a dream of suddenly growing
Too intense for war. Ah, under one's dark arms
Something strange-scented falls—when those on earth
Die, there is not even sound;
One is cool and enthralled in the cockpit,
Turned blue by the power of beauty,
In a pale treasure-hole of soft light
Deep in aesthetic contemplation,
Seeing the ponds catch fire
And cast it through ring after ring
Of land: O death in the middle
Of acres of inch-deep water!   Useless

Firing   small arms
Speckles   from the river
Bank   one ninety-millimeter
Misses   far down   wrong petals   gone

It is this detachment,
The honored aesthetic evil,
The greatest sense of power in one's life,
That must be shed in bars, or by whatever
Means, by starvation
Visions in well-stocked pantries:
The moment when the moon sails in between
The tail-booms   the rudders nod   I swing
Over   directly over the heart
The *heart* of the fire. A mosquito burns out on my cheek
With the cold of my face   there are the eyes
In blue light   bar light
All masked but them   the moon
Crossing from left to right   in the streams below
Oriental fish form quickly
In the chemical shine,
In their eyes one tiny seed
Of deranged, Old Testament light.

Letting go   letting go
The plane rises gently   dark forms
Glide off me   long water   pales
In safe zones   a new cry enters
The voice box of chained family dogs

We buck   leap over something
Not there   settle back
Leave it   leave it clinging and crying
It consumes them in a hot
Body-flash, old age or menopause
Of children, clings and burns
                              eating through
And when a reed mat catches fire
From me, it explodes through field after field
Bearing its sleeper   another

Bomb finds a home
And clings to it like a child. And so

Goodbye to the grassy mountains
To cloud streaming from the night engines
Flags   pennons   curved silks
Of air   myself streaming also
My body covered
With flags, the air of flags
Between the engines.
Forever I do sleep in that position,
Forever in a turn
For home that breaks out streaming banners
From my wingtips,
Wholly in position to admire.

O then I knock it off
And turn for home over the black complex thread worked through
The silver night-sea,
Following the huge, moon-washed steppingstones
Of the Ryukyus south,
The nightgrass of mountains billowing softly
In my rising heat.
                    Turn and tread down
The yellow stones of the islands

To where Okinawa burns,
Pure gold, on the radar screen,
Beholding, beneath, the actual island form
In the vast water-silver poured just above solid ground,
An inch of water extending for thousands of miles
Above flat ploughland. Say "down," and it is done.

All this, and I am still hungry,
Still twenty years overweight, still unable
To get down there or see
What really happened.
                              But it may be that I could not,
If I tried, say to any
Who lived there, deep in my flames: say, in cold
Grinning sweat, as to another
As these homeowners who are always curving
Near me down the different-grassed street: say
As though to the neighbor
I borrowed the hedge-clippers from
On the darker-grassed side of the two,
Come in, my house is yours, come in
If you can, if you
Can pass this unfired door. It is that I can imagine
At the threshold nothing
With its ears crackling off
Like powdery leaves,
Nothing with children of ashes, nothing not
Amiable, gentle, well-meaning,
A little nervous for no
Reason   a little worried   a little too loud
Or too easygoing   nothing I haven't lived with
For twenty years, still nothing not as
American as I am, and proud of it.

Absolution? Sentence? No matter;
The thing itself is in that.

DENISE LEVERTOV *b.* 1923

Losing Track

Long after you have swung back
away from me
I think you are still with me:

you come in close to the shore
on the tide
and nudge me awake the way

a boat adrift nudges the pier:
am I a pier
half-in-half-out of the water?

and in the pleasure of that communion
I lose track,
the moon I watch goes down, the

tide swings you away before
I know I'm
along again long since,

mud sucking at gray and black
timbers of me,
a light growth of green dreams drying.

LOUIS SIMPSON *b.* 1923

Carentan O Carentan

Trees in the old days used to stand
And shape a shady lane
Where lovers wandered hand in hand
Who came from Carentan.

This was the shining green canal
Where we came two by two
Walking at combat-interval.
Such trees we never knew.

The day was early June, the ground
Was soft and bright with dew.
Far away the guns did sound,
But here the sky was blue.

The sky was blue, but there a smoke
Hung still above the sea
Where the ships together spoke
To towns we could not see.

Could you have seen us through a glass
You would have said a walk
Of farmers out to turn the grass,
Each with his own hay-fork.

The watchers in their leopard suits
Waited till it was time,
And aimed between the belt and boot
And let the barrel climb.

I must lie down at once there is
A hammer at my knee.
And call it death or cowardice,
Don't count again on me.

Everything's alright, Mother,
Everyone gets the same
At one time or another.
It's all in the game.

I never strolled, nor ever shall,
Down such a leafy lane.
I never drank in a canal,
Nor ever shall again.

There is a whistling in the leaves
And it is not the wind,
The twigs are falling from the knives
That cut men to the ground.

Tell me, Master-Sergeant,
The way to turn and shoot.
But the Sergeant's silent
That taught me how to do it.

O Captain, show us quickly
Our place upon the map.
But the Captain's sickly
And taking a long nap.

Lieutenant, what's my duty,
My place in the platoon?
He too's a sleeping beauty,
Charmed by that strange tune.

Carentan O Carentan
Before we met with you
We never yet had lost a man
Or known what death could do.

PAUL BLACKBURN *b.* 1926

Málaga: port

It saves the city

a provincial other
wise
port, how the bloody
ships come in, the sheer
machinery of docking, in-
            (how we knock the other larger
       ports to the north, Cádiz and Huelva to the west

loading certain hatches
creak of crane, the strain of ropes, the rub of hulls, that close
smell of sea-rotted wood

and the wine inshore in bars we'll come to later, not
any dream of release but real
                              cold
                                   and flowing
release we cannot beg or steal, but come to later
nub of skulls on hillsides, sweating bodies, gypsies
under the bridge on beds of caña, closed?
                              open mouths of bitches   dull
strain of guitars below, the bold song rising, the hips
rising and the swing of the bloody knockers
steers the world back home   .

ROBERT BLY *b.* 1926

Romans Angry about the Inner World

What shall the world do with its children?
There are lives the executives
Know nothing of,
A leaping of the body,
The body rolling—and I have felt it—
And we float
Joyfully on the dark places;
But the executioners
Move toward Drusia. They tie her legs
On the iron horse. "Here is a woman
Who has seen our mother
In the other world!" Next they warm
The hooks. The two Romans had put their trust
In the outer world. Irons glowed
Like teeth. They wanted her
To assure them. She refused. Finally they took burning
Pine sticks, and pushed them
Into her sides. Her breath rose
And she died. The executioners
Rolled her off onto the ground.

A light snow began to fall
And covered the mangled body,
And the executives, astonished, withdrew.
The other world is like a thorn
In the ear of a tiny beast!
The fingers of the executive are too thick
To pull it out!
It is like a jagged stone
Flying toward them out of the darkness.

ROBERT CREELEY *b.* 1926

The Riddle

What it is, the literal size
incorporates.
                    The question
is a mute question. One is
too lonely, one wants
to stop there, at the edge of

conception. The woman

imperative, the man
lost in stern
thought:

give it form certainly,
the name and titles.

Kore

As I was walking
    I came upon
chance walking
    the same road upon.

As I sat down
   by chance to move
later
   if and as I might,

light the wood was,
   light and green,
and what I saw
   before I had not seen.

It was a lady
   accompanied
by goat men
   leading her.

Her hair held earth.
   Her eyes were dark.
A double flute
   made her move.

"O love,
   where are you
leading
   me now?"

The Window

There will be no simple
way to avoid what
confronts me. Again and
again I know it, but

take heart, hopefully,
in the world unavoidably
present. Here, I think,
is a day, not *a*
but *the*. My hands are

shaking, there is
an insistent tremble
from the night's
drinking. But what

was I after, you
were surely open to me.
Out the far window
there was such intensity

of yellow light. But love,
love I so wanted I
got, didn't I, and then
fell senseless, with relief.

ALLEN GINSBERG *b.* 1926

FROM *KADDISH*
for Naomi Ginsberg 1894–1956

Proem: I

Strange now to think of you, gone without corsets & eyes, while I walk
    on the sunny pavement of Greenwich Village.
downtown Manhattan, clear winter noon, and I've been up all night,
    talking, talking, reading the Kaddish aloud, listening to Ray
    Charles blues shout blind on the phonograph
the rhythm the rhythm — and your memory in my head three years
    after — And read Adonais' last triumphant stanzas aloud —
    wept, realizing how we suffer —
And how Death is that remedy all singers dream of, sing, remember,
    prophesy as in the Hebrew Anthem, or the Buddhist Book of
    Answers — and my own imagination of a withered leaf — at
    dawn —
Dreaming back thru life, Your time — and mine accelerating toward
    Apocalypse,
the final moment — the flower burning in the Day — and what comes
    after,
looking back on the mind itself that saw an American city
a flash away, and the great dream of Me or China, or you and a
    phantom Russia, or a crumpled bed that never existed —
like a poem in the dark — escaped back to Oblivion —

No more to say, and nothing to weep for but the Beings in the Dream,
    trapped in its disappearance,
sighing, screaming with it, buying and selling pieces of phantom, wor-
    shipping each other,
worshipping the God included in it all — longing or inevitability? —
    while it lasts, a Vision — anything more?
It leaps about me, as I go out and walk the street, look back over my
    shoulder, Seventh Avenue, the battlements of window office
    buildings shouldering each other high, under a cloud, tall as
    the sky an instant — and the sky above — an old blue place.
or down the Avenue to the South, to — as I walk toward the Lower
    East Side — where you walked 50 years ago, little girl — from
    Russia, eating the first poisonous tomatoes of America —
    frightened on the dock —
then struggling in the crowds of Orchard Street toward what? —
    toward Newark —
toward candy store, first home-made sodas of the century, hand-
    churned ice cream in backroom on musty brownfloor
    boards —
Toward education marriage nervous breakdown, operation, teaching
    school, and learning to be mad, in a dream — what is this
    life?
Toward the Key in the window — and the great Key lays its head of
    light on top of Manhattan, and over the floor, and lays down
    on the sidewalk — in a single vast beam, moving, as I walk
    down First toward the Yiddish Theater — and the place of
    poverty
you knew, and I know, but without caring now — Strange to have
    moved thru Paterson, and the West, and Europe and here
    again,
with the cries of Spaniards now in the doorstoops doors and dark boys
    on the street, fire escapes old as you
— Tho you're not old now, that's left here with me —
Myself, anyhow, maybe as old as the universe — and I guess that dies
    with us — enough to cancel all that comes — What came is
    gone forever every time —
That's good! That leaves it open for no regret — no fear radiators,
    lacklove, torture even toothache in the end —
Though while it comes it is a lion that eats the soul — and the lamb,
    the soul, in us, alas, offering itself in sacrifice to change's

fierce hunger — hair and teeth — and the roar of bonepain,
skull bare, break rib, rot-skin, braintricked Implacability.

Ai! ai! we do worse! We are in a fix! And you're out, Death let you
out, Death had the Mercy, you're done with your century,
done with God, done with the path thru it — Done with
yourself at last — Pure — Back to the Babe dark before your
Father, before us all — before the world —

There, rest. No more suffering for you. I know where you've gone, it's
good.

No more flowers in the summer fields of New York, no joy now, no
more fear of Louis,

and no more of his sweetness and glasses, his high school decades,
debts, loves, frightened telephone calls, conception beds,
relatives, hands —

No more of sister Elanor, — she gone before you — we kept it secret
— you killed her — or she killed herself to bear with you —
an arthritic heart — But Death's killed you both — No
matter —

Nor your memory of your mother, 1915 tears in silent movies weeks
and weeks — forgetting, agrieve watching Marie Dressler
address humanity, Chaplin dance in youth,

or Boris Godunov, Chaliapin's at the Met, halling his voice of a weeping Czar — by standing room with Elanor & Max — watching also the Capitalists take seats in Orchestra, white furs,
diamonds,

with the YPSL's hitch-hiking thru Pennsylvania, in black baggy gym
skirts pants, photograph of 4 girls holding each other round
the waist, and laughing eye, too coy, virginal solitude of
1920

all girls grown old, or dead, now, and that long hair in the grave —
lucky to have husbands later —

You made it — I came too — Eugene my brother before (still grieving
now and will gream on to his last stiff hand, as he goes thru
his cancer — or kill — later perhaps — soon he will think —)

And it's the last moment I remember, which I see them all, thru
myself, now — tho not you

I didn't foresee what you felt — what more hideous gape of bad
mouth came first — to you — and were you prepared?

To go where? In that Dark — that — in that God? a radiance? A Lord
in the Void? Like an eye in the black cloud in a dream?
Adonoi at last, with you?

Beyond my remembrance! Incapable to guess! Not merely the yellow
  skull in the grave, or a box of worm dust, and a stained
  ribbon — Deathshead with Halo? can you believe it?
Is it only the sun that shines once for the mind, only the flash of
  existence, than none ever was?
Nothing beyond what we have — what you had — that so pitiful —
  yet Triumph,
to have been here, and changed, like a tree, broken, or flower — fed
  to the ground — but mad, with its petals, colored, thinking
  Great Universe, shaken, cut in the head, leaf stript, hid in an
  egg crate hospital, cloth wrapped, sore — freaked in the
  moon brain, Naughtless.
No flower like that flower, which knew itself in the garden, and
  fought the knife — lost
Cut down by an idiot Snowman's icy — even in the Spring — strange
  ghost thought — some Death — Sharp icicle in his hand —
  crowned with old roses — a dog for his eyes — cock of a
  sweatshop — heart of electric irons.
All the accumulations of life, that wear us out — clocks, bodies, con-
  sciousness, shoe, breasts — begotten sons — your Commu-
  nism — ' Paranoia ' into hospitals.
You once kicked Elanor in the leg, she died of heart failure later. You
  of stroke. Asleep? within a year, the two of you, sisters in
  death. Is Elanor happy?
Max grieves alive in an office on Lower Broadway, lone large mustache
  over midnight Accountings, not sure. His life passes — as he
  sees — and what does he doubt now? Still dream of making
  money, or that might have made money, hired nurse, had
  children, found even your Immortality, Naomi?
I'll see him soon. Now I've got to cut through — to talk to you — as I
  didn't when you had a mouth.
Forever. And we're bound for that, Forever — like Emily Dickinson's
  horses — headed to the End.
They know the way — These Steeds — run faster than we think — it's
  our own life they cross — and take with them.

    Magnificent, mourned no more, marred of heart, mind be-
hind, married dreamed, mortal changed — Ass and face done with
murder.
    In the world, given, flower maddened, made no Utopia, shut
under pine, almed in Earth, balmed in Lone, Jehovah, accept.

Nameless, One Faced, Forever beyond me, beginningless, endless, Father in death. Tho I am not there for this Prophecy, I am unmarried, I'm hymnless, I'm Heavenless, headless in blisshood I would still adore

Thee, Heaven, after Death, only One blessed in Nothingness, not light or darkness, Dayless Eternity —

Take this, this Psalm, from me, burst from my hand in a day, some of my Time, now given to Nothing — to praise Thee — But Death

This is the end, the redemption from Wilderness, way for the Wonderer, House sought for All, black handkerchief washed clean by weeping — page beyond Psalm — Last change of mine and Naomi — to God's perfect Darkness — Death, stay thy phantoms!

W. D. SNODGRASS b. 1926

FROM Heart's Needle

6

Easter has come around
again; the river is rising
over the thawed ground
and the banksides. When you come you bring
an egg dyed lavender.
We shout along our bank to hear
our voices returning from the hills to meet us.
We need the landscape to repeat us.

You lived on this bank first.
While nine months filled your term, we knew
how your lungs, immersed
in the womb, miraculously grew
their useless folds till
the fierce, cold air rushed in to fill
them out like bushes thick with leaves. You took your hour,
caught breath, and cried with your full lung power.

Over the stagnant bight
we see the hungry bank swallow
    flaunting his free flight
still; we sink in mud to follow
    the killdeer from the grass
that hides her nest. That March there was
rain; the rivers rose; you could hear killdeers flying
    all night over the mudflats crying.

You bring back how the red-
winged blackbird shrieked, slapping frail wings,
    diving at my head—
I saw where her tough nest, cradled, swings
    in tall reeds that must sway
with the winds blowing every way.
If you recall much, you recall this place. You still
    live nearby—on the opposite hill.

After the sharp windstorm
of July Fourth, all that summer
    through the gentle, warm
afternoons, we heard great chain saws chirr
    like iron locusts. Crews
of roughneck boys swarmed to cut loose
branches wrenched in the shattering wind, to hack free
    all the torn limbs that could sap the tree.

In the debris lay
starlings, dead. Near the park's birdrun
    we surprised one day
a proud, tan-spatted, buff-brown pigeon.
    In my hand she flapped so
fearfully that I let her go.
Her keeper came. And we helped snarl her in a net.
    You bring things I'd as soon forget.

You raise into my head
a Fall night that I came once more
    to sit on your bed;
sweat beads stood out on your arms and fore-
    head and you wheezed for breath,
for help, like some child caught beneath

its comfortable woolly blankets, drowning there.
　　Your lungs caught and would not take the air.

　　　Of all things, only we
　have power to choose that we should die;
　　　nothing else is free
　in this world to refuse it. Yet I,
　　　who say this, could not raise
　myself from bed how many days
to the thieving world. Child, I have another wife,
　another child. We try to choose our life.

　　　　　　　7

　Here in the scuffled dust
　　is our ground of play.
　I lift you on your swing and must
　　shove you away,
　see you return again,
　　drive you off again, then

　stand quiet till you come.
　　You, though you climb
　higher, farther from me, longer,
　　will fall back to me stronger.
　Bad penny, pendulum,
　　you keep my constant time

　to bob in blue July
　　where fat goldfinches fly
　over the glittering, fecund
　　reach of our growing lands.
　Once more now, this second,
　　I hold you in my hands.

GALWAY KINNELL *b.* 1927

Vapor Trail Reflected in the Frog Pond

1

The old watch: their
thick eyes
puff and foreclose by the moon. The young, heads
trailed by the beginnings of necks,
shiver,
in the guarantee they shall be bodies.

In the frog pond
the vapor of a SAC bomber creeps,

I hear its drone, drifting, high up
in immaculate ozone.

2

And I hear,
coming over the hills, America singing,
her varied carols I hear:
crack of deputies' rifles practicing their aim on stray dogs at night,
sput of cattleprod,
TV groaning at the smells of the human body,
curses of the soldier as he poisons, burns, grinds, and stabs
the rice of the world,
with open mouth, crying strong, hysterical curses.

3

And by rice paddies in Asia
bones
wearing a few shadows
walk down a dirt road, smashed
bloodsuckers on their heel, knowing
the flesh a man throws down in the sunshine
dogs shall eat

and the flesh that is upthrown in the air
shall be seized by birds,
shoulder blades smooth, unmarked by old feather-holes,
hands rivered
by blue, erratic wanderings of the blood,
eyes crinkled up
as they gaze up at the drifting sun that gave us our lives,
seed dazzled over the footbattered blaze of the earth.

W. S. MERWIN *b.* 1927

Bell Buoy

So we set signs over the world to say
To ourselves, returning, that we know the place,
Marking the sea too with shaped tokens
Of our usage, which even while they serve us
Make one with the unmeasured mist, sea-slap,
Green rock awash with the gray heave just
Out of sight, wet air saturated with sounds
But no breath—and in no time they are seen
To be in league with the world's remoteness
Whose features we grope for through fog and can never
Seize to our satisfaction. First the sound
Comes, and again, from the caged bell lost in the gray
Out ahead. Then into the glasses,
And gone, and again sighted, staying:
A black shape like nothing, rounded, rocking like
A chair, with a gull on top. Clearer
The dreaming bronze clangs over the lifting
Swell, through the fog-drift, clangs, not
On the sea-stroke but on the fifth second clangs,
Recalling something, out of some absence
We cannot fathom, with itself communing.
Was it we who made this, or the sea's necessity?
You can hear the wash on its rolling plates
Over your own wake, as you come near

And confirm: black can, odd number crusted
Already with gull crap over the new paint,
Green beard and rust speckling its undersides
As you see when it rolls. Nothing you can
Say as you pass, though there are only you two
And you come so close and seem to share
So much. And it will twist and stare after you
Through the closing fog, clanging. It is
A dead thing but we have agreed upon it: kept
To port, entering, starboard departing, as
May your fortune be, it can assure you
Of where you are, though it knows nothing
Of where you are going or may have been.

JAMES WRIGHT *b.* 1927

A *Blessing*

Just off the highway to Rochester, Minnesota,
Twilight bounds softly forth on the grass.
And the eyes of those two Indian ponies
Darken with kindness.
They have come gladly out of the willows
To welcome my friend and me.
We step over the barbed wire into the pasture
Where they have been grazing all day, alone.
They ripple tensely, they can hardly contain their happiness
That we have come.
They bow shyly as wet swans. They love each other.
There is no loneliness like theirs.
At home once more,
They begin munching the young tufts of spring in the darkness.
I would like to hold the slenderer one in my arms,
For she has walked over to me
And nuzzled my left hand.
She is black and white,
Her mane falls wild on her forehead,

And the light breeze moves me to caress her long ear
That is delicate as the skin over a girl's wrist.
Suddenly I realize
That if I stepped out of my body I would break
Into blossom.

DONALD HALL *b.* 1928

The Snow

Snow is in the oak.
Behind the thick, whitening
air which the wind drives,
the weight of the sun
presses the snow
on the pane of my window.

I remember snows and my walking
through their first fall in cities,
asleep or drunk
with the slow, desperate falling.
The snow blurs in my eyes
with other snows.

Snow is what must
come down, even if it struggles
to stay in the air with the strength
of the wind. Like an old man,
whatever I touch I turn
to the story of death.

Snow is what fills
the oak, and what covers
the grass and the bare garden.
Snow is what reverses
the sidewalk and the lawn
into the substance of whiteness.

So the watcher sleeps himself
back to the baby's eyes.
The tree, the breast, and the floor
are limbs of him, and from
his eyes he extends a skin
which grows over the world.

The baby is what must
have fallen, like snow. He resisted,
the way the old man
struggles inside the airy tent
to keep on breathing.
Birth is the fear of death.

Snow is what melts.
I cannot open the door
to the cycles of water.
The sun has withdrawn itself
and the snow keeps falling,
and something will always be falling.

ANNE SEXTON *b.* 1928

You, Doctor Martin

You, Doctor Martin, walk
from breakfast to madness. Late August
I speed through the antiseptic tunnel
where the moving dead still talk
of pushing their bones against the thrust
of cure. And I am queen of this summer hotel
or the laughing bee on a stalk

of death. We stand in broken
lines and wait while they unlock
the door and count us at the frozen gates
of dinner. The shibboleth is spoken
and we move to gravy in our smock

of smiles. We chew in rows, our plates
scratch and whine like chalk

in school. There are no knives
for cutting your throat. I make
moccasins all morning. At first my hands
kept empty, unraveled for the lives
they used to work. Now I learn to take
them back, each angry finger that demands
I mend what another will break

tomorrow. Of course, I love you;
you lean above the plastic sky,
god of our block, prince of all the foxes.
The breaking crowns are new
that Jack wore. Your third eye
Moves among us and lights the separate boxes
where we sleep or cry.

What large children we are
here. All over I grow most tall
in the best ward. Your business is people,
you call at the madhouse, an oracular
eye in our nest. Out in the hall
the intercom pages you. You twist in the pull
of the foxy children who fall

like floods of life in frost.
And we are magic talking to itself,
noisy and alone. I am queen of all my sins
forgotten. Am I still lost?
Once I was beautiful. Now I am myself,
counting this row and that row of moccasins
waiting on the silent shelf.

The Starry Night

*That does not keep me from having a terrible need of—shall
I say the word—religion. Then I go out at night to paint the
stars.*

—VINCENT VAN GOGH in a letter to his brother

The town does not exist
except where one black-haired tree slips
up like a drowned woman into the hot sky.
The town is silent. The night boils with eleven stars.
Oh starry starry night! This is how
I want to die.

It moves. They are all alive.
Even the moon bulges in its orange irons
to push children, like a god, from its eye.
The old unseen serpent swallows up the stars.
Oh starry starry night! This is how
I want to die:

into that rushing beast of the night,
sucked up by that great dragon, to split
from my life with no flag,
no belly,
no cry.

GARY SNYDER *b.* 1930

FROM *Logging*

1

The morning star is not a star
Two seedling fir, one died
                        Io, Io,
Girdled in wistaria
Wound with ivy
                "The May Queen
Is the survival of
A pre-human
Rutting season"

The year`spins
Pleiades sing to their rest

at San Francisco
dream
dream
Green comes out of the ground
Birds squabble
Young girls run mad with the pine bough,
                                        Io

4

Pines, under pines,
            Seami Motokiyo
            The Doer stamps his foot.
            A thousand board-feet
Bucked, skidded, loaded—
(Takasago, Ise) float in a mill pond;
A thousand years dancing
Flies in the saw kerf.

Cliff by Tomales Bay
Seal's slick head
            head shoulders breasts
            glowing in night saltwater
Skitter of fish, and above, behind the pines,
Bear grunts, stalking the Pole-star.

Foot-whack on polished boards
Slide and stop; drum-thump.
"Today's wind moves in the pines"
                        falling
And skidding the red-bark pine.
Clouds over Olallie Butte
Scatter rain on the Schoolie flat.
A small bear slips out the wet brush
                        crosses the creek
Seami, Kwanami,
            Gone too.
Through the pines.

8

Each dawn is clear
Cold air bites the throat.

Thick frost on the pine bough
Leaps from the tree
     snapped by the diesel

Drifts and glitters in the
     horizontal sun.
In the frozen grass
     smoking boulders
     ground by steel tracks.
In the frozen grass
     wild horses stand
     beyond a row of pines.
The D8 tears through piss-fir,
Scrapes the seed-pine
     chipmunks flee,
A black ant carries an egg
Aimlessly from the battered ground.
Yellowjackets swarm and circle
Above the crushed dead log, their home.
Pitch oozes from barked
     trees still standing,
Mashed bushes make strange smells.
Lodgepole pines are brittle.
Camprobbers flutter to watch.

A few stumps, drying piles of brush;
Under the thin duff, a toe-scrape down
Black lava of a late flow.
Leaves stripped from thornapple
Taurus by nightfall.

SYLVIA PLATH 1932–1963

Daddy

You do not do, you do not do
Any more, black shoe
In which I have lived like a foot

For thirty years, poor and white,
Barely daring to breathe or Achoo!

Daddy, I have had to kill you.
You died before I had time—
Marble-heavy, a bag full of God,
Ghastly statue with one grey toe
Big as a Frisco seal

And a head in the freakish Atlantic
Where it pours bean green over blue
In the waters off beautiful Nauset.
I used to pray to recover you.
Ach, du!

In the German tongue, in the Polish town
Scraped flat by the roller
Of wars, wars, wars.
But the name of the town is common.
My Polack friend

Says there are a dozen or two.
So I never could tell where you
Put your foot, your root,
I never could talk to you.
The tongue stuck in my jaw.

It stuck in a barb wire snare.
Ich, ich, ich, ich!
I could hardly speak.
I thought every German was you.
And the language obscene

An engine, an engine
Chuffing me off like a Jew.
A Jew to Dachau, Auschwitz, Belsen.
I began to talk like a Jew.
I think I may well be a Jew.

The snows of the Tyrol, the clear beer of Vienna
Are not very pure or true.
With my gypsy ancestress and my weird luck

And my Tarot pack and my Tarot pack
I may be a bit of a Jew.

I have always been scared of *you*,
With your Luftwaffe, your gobbledygoo.
And your neat moustache
And your Aryan eye, bright blue.
Panzer-man, panzer-man, o You!

Not God but a swastika
So black no sky could squeak through.
Every woman adores a Fascist,
The boot in the face, the brute
Brute heart of a brute like you.

You stand at the blackboard, daddy,
In the picture I have of you,
A cleft in your chin instead of your foot
But no less a devil for that, no not
Any less the black man who

Bit my pretty red heart in two.
I was ten when they buried you.
At twenty I tried to die
And get back, back, back to you.
I thought even the bones would do.

But they pulled me out of the sack,
And they stuck me together with glue.
And then I knew what to do.
I made a model of you,
A man in black with a Meinkampf look

And a love of the rack and the screw.
And I said I do, I do.
So daddy, I'm finally through.
The black telephone's off at the root,
The voices just can't worm through.

If I've killed one man, I've killed two—
The vampire who said he was you
And drank my blood for a year—

Seven years, if you want to know.
Daddy, you can lie back now.

There's a stake in your fat black heart
And the villagers never liked you.
They are dancing and stamping on you.
They always *knew* it was you.
Daddy, daddy, you bastard, I'm through.

Death & Co.

Two, of course there are two.
It seems perfectly natural now—
The one who never looks up, whose eyes are lidded
And balled, like Blake's,
Who exhibits

The birthmarks that are his trademark—
The scald scar of water,
The nude
Verdigris of the condor.
I am red meat. His beak

Claps sidewise: I am not his yet.
He tells me how badly I photograph.
He tells me how sweet
The babies look in their hospital
Icebox, a simple

Frill at the neck,
Then the flutings of their Ionian
Death-gowns,
Then two little feet.
He does not smile or smoke.

The other does that,
His hair long and plausive.
Bastard
Masturbating a glitter,
He wants to be loved.

I do not stir.
The frost makes a flower,
The dew makes a star,
The dead bell,
The dead bell.

Somebody's done for.

Ariel

Stasis in darkness.
Then the substanceless blue
Pour of tor and distances.

God's lioness,
How one we grow,
Pivot of heels and knees!—The furrow

Splits and passes, sister to
The brown arc
Of the neck I cannot catch,

Nigger-eye
Berries cast dark
Hooks—

Black sweet blood mouthfuls,
Shadows.
Something else

Hauls me through air—
Thighs, hair;
Flakes from my heels.

White
Godiva, I unpeel—
Dead hands, dead stringencies.

And now I
Foam to wheat, a glitter of seas.
The child's cry

Melts in the wall.
And I
Am the arrow,

The dew that flies
Suicidal, at one with the drive
Into the red

Eye, the cauldron of morning.

LeROI JONES *b.* 1934

An Agony. As Now.

I am inside someone
who hates me. I look
out from his eyes. Smell
what fouled tunes come in
to his breath. Love his
wretched women.

Slits in the metal, for sun. Where
my eyes sit turning, at the cool air
the glance of light, or hard flesh
rubbed against me, a woman, a man,
without shadow, or voice, or meaning.

This is the enclosure (flesh,
where innocence is a weapon. An
abstraction. Touch. (Not mine.
Or yours, if you are the soul I had
and abandoned when I was blind and had
my enemies carry me as a dead man
(if he is beautiful, or pitied.

It can be pain. (As now, as all his
flesh hurts me.) It can be that. Or
pain. As when she ran from me into

that forest.
                        Or pain, the mind
silver spiraled whirled against the
sun, higher than even old men thought
God would be. Or pain. And the other. The
yes. (Inside his books, his fingers. They
are withered yellow flowers and were never
beautiful.) The yes. You will, lost soul, say
'beauty.' Beauty, practiced, as the tree. The
slow river. A white sun in its wet sentences.
Or, the cold men in their gale. Ecstasy. Flesh
or soul. The yes. (Their robes blown. Their bowls
empty. They chant at my heels, not at yours.) Flesh
or soul, as corrupt. Where the answer moves too quickly.
Where the God is a self, after all.)

Cold air blown through narrow blind eyes. Flesh,
white hot metal. Glows as the day with its sun.
It is a human love, I live inside. A bony skeleton
you recognize as words or simple feeling.

But it has no feeling. As the metal, is hot, it is not,
given to love.

It burns the thing
inside it. And that thing
screams.

Notes on the Poets

THE FOLLOWING NOTES on the poets represented in this anthology are
intended to provide only a minimal identification of them and a highly
selective list of their books of poems.

Dannie Abse, WELSH, b. 1923. London physician; playwright, anthologist,
leader of "Maverick" group, journalist (medical correspondent). *Ten-
ants of the House*, 1957; *Poems Golders Green*, 1962.

A. Alvarez, ENGLISH, b. 1929. Critic, journalist, poetry editor of *The Ob-
server*; occasional visiting professor. Outstanding English advocate of
"extremist" confessional poetry after the manner of Robert Lowell, as
opposed to the "Movement" poetry represented in the anthologies of
Robert Conquest.

Brother Antoninus (William Everson), AMERICAN, b. 1912. Dominican
lay brother associated with San Francisco "Beat" movement in certain
ways, but mostly a poetic disciple of Robinson Jeffers. *The Residual
Years*, 1948; *The Crooked Lines of God*, 1959; *The Hazards of Holiness*, 1963; *The Rose of Solitude*, 1967.

John Berryman, AMERICAN, b. 1914. University professor, critic, short-story
writer, biographer. *The Dispossessed*, 1948; *Homage to Mistress Brad-
street*, 1959; *77 Dream Songs*, 1964; *Berryman's Sonnets*, 1967.

Elizabeth Bishop, AMERICAN, b. 1911. For many years resident in Brazil.
North and South, 1946; *Poems*, 1955; *Question of Travel*, 1965.

Paul Blackburn, AMERICAN, b. 1926. Editor, translator, associated with
"Black Mountain" poets. *The Dissolving Fabric*, 1955.

Robert Bly, AMERICAN, b. 1926. Translator; editor, *The Sixties*; associated
with Donald Hall, Louis Simpson, James Wright, and James Dickey
in attempts to infuse a poetry of extreme simplicity with "surrealist"
techniques borrowed from Lorca and other European models. *Silence
in the Snowy Fields*, 1962; *The Light around the Body*, 1967.

Hayden Carruth, AMERICAN, 1921. Critic, editor, novelist. *The Crow and
the Hearth*, 1959; *The Norfolk Poems*, 1963; *Nothing for Tigers*, 1965.

Austin Clarke, IRISH, b. 1896. Dean of Irish poets, playwright, journalist;
was younger associate of Yeats in Abbey Theatre. *Collected Poems*,

1935; *Later Poems*, 1961; *Flight to Africa*, 1963; *Mnemosyne Lay in Dust*, 1966.

Robert Creeley, AMERICAN, b. 1926. University teacher, novelist, former editor of *Black Mountain Review*. *For Love: Poems 1950–1960*, 1962; *Words*, 1967.

Donald Davie, ENGLISH, b. 1922. Critic, university professor, translator. *Brides of Reason*, 1955; *A Winter Talent*, 1957; *New and Selected Poems*, 1961; *Events and Wisdoms*, 1964.

Denis Devlin, IRISH, 1908–1959. Diplomat, translator. *Selected Poems*, 1963, *Collected Poems*, 1964.

James Dickey, AMERICAN, b. 1923. Former advertising executive. Night fighter pilot in World War II and Korea. *Poems 1957–1967*, 1967.

Robert Duncan, AMERICAN, b. 1919. Critic, editor, estheticist-mystic associated with Black Mountain group; experimenter with collage-like structures in longer works. *Letters*, 1958; *Selected Poems*, 1959; *The Opening of the Field*, 1960; *Roots and Branches*, 1964.

D. J. Enright, ENGLISH, b. 1920. University professor, critic, translator, anthologist, novelist; extensive experience in Far East. *The Laughing Hyena*, 1953; *Bread Rather than Blossoms*, 1956; *Some Men Are Brothers*, 1960; *Addictions*, 1962; *The Old Adam*, 1965.

Lawrence Ferlinghetti, AMERICAN, b. 1919. Publisher of City Lights Books, translator, an original participant in San Francisco "Beat" movement contributing sophisticated notes related to the work of modern poets in France, where he studied for a doctorate. Now primarily a political satirist in his poetry and plays. *Pictures of the Gone World*, 1955; *A Coney Island of the Mind*, 1958; *Routines*, 1964.

Ian Hamilton Finlay, SCOTTISH, b. 1925. Edinburgh poet, typographer, and designer, associated with Concretist movement in poetry. Former road laborer, farm worker; publisher of Wild Hawthorn Press, editor of *Poor. Old. Tired. Horse. The Dancers Inherit the Party*, 1962; *Telegrams from My Windmill*, 1964.

Allen Ginsberg, AMERICAN, b. 1926. Best-known, and probably most accomplished, of the "Beat" poets. *Howl*, 1956; *Empty Mirror*, 1960; *Kaddish*, 1960; *Reality Sandwiches*, 1963; *Jukebox All'Idrogeno*, 1965.

Paul Goodman, AMERICAN, b. 1911. Outstanding nonconformist thinker and social critic; author of studies in city planning, *Gestalt* psychotherapy, esthetic theory, and adolescents' problems in the United States. Lay analyst. Novelist. *The Lordly Hudson*, 1962; *Hawkweed*, 1967.

W. S. Graham, SCOTTISH, b. 1917. Employed by coast guard in Cornwall, where he lives in seclusion from literary world. *The Seven Journeys*, 1944; *Second Poems*, 1945; *The White Threshold*, 1949; *The Nightfishing*, 1955.

Thom Gunn, ENGLISH, b. 1929. University teacher, critic, anthologist; has lived in California since 1954. *Fighting Terms*, 1954; *The Sense of Movement*, 1957; *My Sad Captains*, 1961; *Touch*, 1967.

Ramon Guthrie, AMERICAN, b. 1896. Professor of French (retired), critic, translator. Member of the literary generation of the twenties and early thirties, in Paris and the United States, who re-emerged with *Graffiti*, 1959.

Donald Hall, AMERICAN, b. 1928. Professor, anthologist, critic; poetry editor for nine years of *Paris Review*; associated with *Sixties* group. *Exiles and Marriages*, 1955; *The Dark Houses*, 1958; *A Roof of Tiger Lilies*, 1964.

Michael Hamburger, BRITISH, b. 1924. Born in Germany, came with family to Britain as refugees in 1933. University teacher; German scholar and translator, critic, short-story writer. *Flowering Cactus*, 1950; *Poems*, 1950–1951, 1952; *The Dual Site*, 1958; *Weather and Season*, 1963.

Ted Hughes, ENGLISH, b. 1930. The outstanding British poet of his generation. Short-story writer; radio and television dramatist. *The Hawk in the Rain*, 1957; *Lupercal*, 1960; *Wodwo*, 1967.

Randall Jarrell, AMERICAN, 1914–1965. Professor, critic, translator, editor, novelist. *Selected Poems*, 1955; *The Woman at the Washington Zoo*, 1960; *The Lost World*, 1965.

Elizabeth Jennings, ENGLISH, b. 1926. Librarian, publisher's reader, anthologist. *Collected Poems*, 1967.

LeRoi Jones, AMERICAN, b. 1934. Editor of *Yugen*, critic, student of jazz, playwright, associated with Black Nationalist movement. *Preface to a Twenty Volume Suicide Note*, 1960; *The Dead Lecturer*, 1964.

Patrick Kavanagh, IRISH, 1905–1967. Earned a difficult livelihood through various means including small farming and journalism; in recent years associated with the group around X magazine, edited in London during its existence by David Wright. *Collected Poems*, 1964.

Galway Kinnell, AMERICAN, b. 1927. Teacher, translator. *What a Kingdom It Was*, 1960; *Flower Herding on Mount Monadnock*, 1964; *Body Rags*, 1967.

Thomas Kinsella, IRISH, b. 1928. Formerly civil servant, Department of Finance; translator; now university professor, resident in United States. *Another September*, 1958; *Poems and Translations*, 1961; *Downstream*, 1962; *Wormwood*, 1967.

Philip Larkin, ENGLISH, b. 1922. University librarian; a poetic spokesman of the literary generation of "angry young men"; novelist. *The North Ship*, 1945; *The Less Deceived*, 1955; *The Whitsun Weddings*, 1964.

Denise Levertov, AMERICAN, b. 1923. British-born; married the novelist Mitchell Goodman and settled in the United States in 1948. Associated with Black Mountain group. Editor, occasional college lecturer. *The Double Image*, 1946; *Here and Now*, 1957; *Overland to the Islands*,

1958; *With Eyes at the Backs of Our Heads*, 1960; *The Jacob's Ladder*, 1961; *O Taste and See*, 1964; *The Sorrow Dance*, 1967.

Robert Lowell, AMERICAN, b. 1917. The outstanding American poet to emerge since World War II, and the chief influence on the "confessional" school. Has taught in various universities. Translator. *Land of Unlikeness*, 1944; *Lord Weary's Castle*, 1946; *The Mills of the Kavanaughs*, 1951; *Life Studies*, 1959; *Imitations*, 1961; *For the Union Dead*, 1964; *The Old Glory* (poetic drama), 1965; *Near the Ocean*, 1967.

George MacBeth, SCOTTISH, b. 1932. BBC talks producer. *The Broken Places*, 1963; *A Doomsday Book*, 1965; *The Colour of Blood*, 1967.

Norman MacCaig, SCOTTISH, b. 1910. Edinburgh schoolmaster. *Riding Lights*, 1956; *The Sinai Sort*, 1957; *A Common Grace*, 1960; *A Round of Applause*, 1962; *Measures*, 1965; *Surroundings*, 1966.

Hugh MacDiarmid (Christopher Grieve), SCOTTISH, b. 1892. The leading modern Scottish poet, rivaled only by Edwin Muir. A Scottish Nationalist and Communist, he opposed the Prime Minister in the general election of 1964, standing in the same constituency. Though his greatest work has been in Scots, a considerable body of his writing in English is not only distinguished but virtually unknown to American readers. *Collected Poems*, 1962.

W. S. Merwin, AMERICAN, b. 1927. Translator, editor, journalist, playwright. *A Mask for Janus*, 1952; *The Dancing Bears*, 1954; *Green with Beasts*, 1956; *The Drunk in the Furnace*, 1960; *The Lice*, 1967.

Christopher Middleton, ENGLISH, b. 1926. University lecturer in German; translator, short story writer, critic, librettist. *Poems*, 1944; *Nocturne in Eden*, 1945; *Torse 3*, 1962; *Nonsequences*, 1965.

John Montague, IRISH, b. 1929. American-born, has divided his time between Ireland (Dublin and Ulster) and living abroad—France, Mexico, the United States. Film critic, journalist, occasional university teacher. *Forms of Exile*, 1958; *Poisoned Lands*, 1961; *All Legendary Obstacles*, 1966; *A Chosen Light*, 1967.

Richard Murphy, IRISH, b. 1927. After British education, returned to Galway, where, among other activities, rebuilt and handles the old-time hooker *Ave Maria* for tourists who wish to go sailing and fishing on it. *The Last Galway Hooker*, 1961; *Sailing to an Island*, 1963.

Howard Nemerov, AMERICAN, b. 1920. Novelist, critic, former coeditor *Furioso*, college teacher. *New and Selected Poems*, 1960; *The Next Room of the Dream*, 1962; *The Blue Swallow*, 1967.

Charles Olson, AMERICAN, b. 1910. Leading theorist of Black Mountain group; his essay on "projective verse" attempts in a way to carry forward William Carlos Williams' conceptions of functional technique, or what Olson calls "composition by field." *The Distances*, 1960; *The Maximus Poems*, 1960; *Selected Writings*, 1966.

Sylvia Plath, AMERICAN, 1932–1963. Wife of the British poet Ted Hughes;

her suicidally intense last poems made an extraordinary impact after her death. *The Colossus*, 1962; *Ariel*, 1965.

Peter Redgrove, ENGLISH, b. 1932. Trained as a scientist, has turned to poetry and teaching. The most vigorous and idiosyncratic poet by far of those associated with "The Group." *The Collector*, 1959; *The Nature of Cold Weather*, 1961; *At the White Monument*, 1963; *The Force and Other Poems*, 1966.

Kenneth Rexroth, AMERICAN, b. 1905. Journalist, critic, translator, associated with various avant-garde movements and West Coast political nonconformism. *In Defense of the Earth*, 1956; *Natural Numbers*, 1963.

Theodore Roethke, AMERICAN, 1908–1963. University professor; in his later years a central figure among poets of the Pacific Northwest while his national and international reputation was rapidly growing. *Collected Poems*, 1966.

Muriel Rukeyser, AMERICAN, b. 1913. College teacher, critic, biographer, translator, cultural historian with a special interest in correlations between scientific theory and esthetic principles. *Waterlily Fire*, 1963; *The Outer Banks*, 1967.

James Schevill, AMERICAN, b. 1920. College professor, Director of Poetry Center (San Francisco State College), playwright, editor, biographer. *Public Dooms and Private Destinations*, 1963; *The Stalingrad Elegies*, 1964.

Delmore Schwartz, AMERICAN, 1913–1966. Editor, college teacher, verse-playwright. *Summer Knowledge*, 1959.

Anne Sexton, AMERICAN, b. 1928. Once for a short time a fashion model; disciple of "confessional" poetic school of Robert Lowell and W. D. Snodgrass. *Selected Poems*, 1964; *Live or Die*, 1967.

Jon Silkin, ENGLISH, b. 1930. Editor, teacher, critic. *The Peaceable Kingdom*, 1954; *The Two Freedoms*, 1958; *The Re-Ordering of the Stones*, 1961.

Louis Simpson, AMERICAN, b. 1923. Professor, critic, fiction writer, associated with "Sixties" group. *Selected Poems*, 1965.

W. D. Snodgrass, AMERICAN, b. 1926. University teacher, translator. *Heart's Needle*, 1959, is especially in the title poem an outstanding example of postwar "confessional" poetry.

Gary Snyder, AMERICAN, b. 1930. Has worked in West Coast logging jobs; resident in Japan for a number of years. *A Range of Poems*, 1966.

William Stafford, AMERICAN, b. 1914. College professor. *West of Your City*, 1960; *Traveling through the Dark*, 1962.

May Swenson, AMERICAN, b. 1919. *Another Animal*, 1954 (in *Poets of Today: I*); *A Cage of Spines*, 1958; *To Mix with Time*, 1963; *Half Sun Half Sleep*, 1967.

R. S. Thomas, WELSH, b. 1913. Welsh priest (vicar of Eglwys Fach);

anthologist. *Stones of the Field,* 1947; *Poetry for Supper,* 1958; *Tares,* 1961; *The Bread of Truth,* 1963.

Charles Tomlinson, ENGLISH, b. 1927. University teacher, strongly influenced by American poetry. *Relations and Contraries,* 1951; *The Necklace,* 1955; *Seeing Is Believing,* 1958; *A Peopled Landscape,* 1963; *American Scenes,* 1966.

Theodore Weiss, AMERICAN, b. 1916. College professor; editor, with Renée Weiss, of *Quarterly Review of Literature. The Catch,* 1951; *Outlanders,* 1960; *Gunsight,* 1964; *The Medium,* 1965.

Richard Wilbur, AMERICAN, b. 1921. College professor, translator. *The Beautiful Changes,* 1947; *Ceremony,* 1950; *Things of This World,* 1956; *Advice to a Prophet,* 1961.

David Wright, BRITISH, b. 1920. Born in South Africa; edited X magazine; translator, anthologist, critic, free-lance writer. *Monologue of a Deaf Man,* 1958; *Adam at Evening,* 1965.

James Wright, AMERICAN, b. 1927. University teacher, member of Sixties group. *The Green Wall,* 1957; *Saint Judas,* 1959; *The Branch Will Not Break,* 1963.

Index of Authors,
Titles, and First Lines